KT-447-436

easy to make!
Salads & Dressings

Good Housekeeping

easy to make!
Salads & Dressings

COLLINS & BROWN

First published in Great Britain in 2008
by Collins & Brown
10 Southcombe Street
London W14 0RA

An imprint of Anova Books Company Ltd

Copyright © The National Magazine Company Limited
and Collins & Brown 2008

All rights reserved. No part of this publication may
be reproduced, stored in a retrieval system, or transmitted in any
form or by any means, electronic, mechanical, photocopying,
recording or otherwise, without the prior written consent of the
copyright holder.

The expression Good Housekeeping as used in the title
of the book is the trademark of the National Magazine Company
and The Hearst Corporation, registered in the United Kingdom
and USA, and other principal countries of the world, and is the
absolute property of The National Magazine Company and The
Hearst Corporation. The use of this trademark other than with
the express permission of The National Magazine Company or
The Hearst Corporation is strictly prohibited.

The Good Housekeeping website is
www.goodhousekeeping.co.uk

1 2 3 4 5 6 7 8 9

ISBN 978-1-84340-462-0

A catalogue record for this book is available from the British
Library.

Reproduction by Dot Gradations Ltd
Printed and bound by SNP Leefung, China

This book can be ordered direct from the publisher. Contact the
marketing department, but try your bookshop first.

www.anovabooks.com

NOTES

- Both metric and imperial measures are given for the recipes. Follow either set of measures, not a mixture of both, as they are not interchangeable.
- All spoon measures are level.
  1 tsp = 5ml spoon; 1 tbsp = 15ml spoon.
- Ovens and grills must be preheated to the specified temperature.
- Use sea salt and freshly ground black pepper unless otherwise suggested.
- Fresh herbs should be used unless dried herbs are specified in a recipe.
- Medium eggs should be used except where otherwise specified. Free-range eggs are recommended.
- Note that certain recipes, including mayonnaise, lemon curd and some cold desserts, contain raw or lightly cooked eggs. The young, elderly, pregnant women and anyone with an immune-deficiency disease should avoid these, because of the slight risk of salmonella.
- Calorie, fat and carbohydrate counts per serving are provided for the recipes.

Picture credits
Photographers: Nicki Dowey; Craig Robertson (all Basics photography)
Stylist: Helen Trent
Home economist: Emma Jane Frost

Contents

Foreword

Salads have become far more varied and extravagant since my first one. That was the one my grandmother made every year on Boxing Day. Perfectly arranged on a large flat plate, there were lettuce leaves around the outside and each inner layer featured a different ingredient, such as sliced tomatoes, cucumbers, radishes and hard-boiled eggs; it was served alongside cold cuts of turkey and ham with a selection of pickles.

Now anything and everything can be thrown together in a salad bowl. Leftovers from a roast chicken? Pop them in with some crisp Cos lettuce leaves, cubes of toasted garlicky bread, a few shavings of Parmesan and you've got a Caesar Salad with a twist. Fancy eggs for supper? Cook them in boiling water until they're still a little runny on the inside, then serve with a warm lentil salad and you have a gourmet supper that wouldn't look out of place in any top-notch restaurant.

Those ideas, plus many more, are among the 101 recipes in this book. They include light, elegant starters and side salads, main-course salads using fish, chicken, meat or beans, and a great selection of quick and easy dressings. All the recipes have been tried, tasted and cooked three times to make sure they look and taste delicious the very first time you make them. Enjoy!

Emma Marsden
Cookery Editor
Good Housekeeping

0

The Basics

Seeding tomatoes

1 Halve the tomato through the core. Use a spoon or a small sharp knife to remove the seeds and juice. Shake off the excess liquid.

2 Chop the tomato as required for your recipe and place in a colander for a minute or two, to drain off any excess liquid.

Peeling tomatoes

1 Fill a bowl or pan with boiling water. Using a slotted spoon, carefully add the tomato and leave for 15–30 seconds, then remove to a chopping board.

2 Use a small sharp knife to cut out the core in a single cone-shaped piece. Discard the core.

3 Peel off the skin; it should come away easily, depending on ripeness.

Preparing tomatoes, avocados and peppers

These colourful Mediterranean vegetables add a rich flavour to salads.

Cutting tomatoes

1 Use a small sharp knife to cut the core out in a single cone-shaped piece. Discard the core.

2 **Wedges** Halve the tomato and then cut into quarters or into three.

3 **Slices** Hold the tomato with the cored side on the chopping board for greater stability and use a serrated knife to cut into slices.

Avocados

Prepare avocados just before serving because their flesh discolours quickly once exposed to air.

1 Halve the avocado lengthways and twist the two halves apart. Tap the stone with a sharp knife, then twist to remove the stone.

2 Run a knife between the flesh and skin and pull away. Slice the flesh.

Seeding peppers

The seeds and white pith of peppers taste bitter so should be removed.

1 Cut off the top of the pepper, then cut away and discard the seeds and white pith.

2 Alternatively, cut the pepper in half vertically and snap out the white pithy core and seeds. Trim away the rest of the white membrane with a knife.

Chargrilling peppers

Charring imparts a smoky flavour and makes peppers easier to peel.

1 Hold the pepper, using tongs, over the gas flame on your hob (or under a preheated grill) until the skin blackens, turning until black all over.

2 Put in a bowl, cover and leave to cool (the steam will help to loosen the skin). Peel.

Chillies

Always wash your hands thoroughly with soap and water immediately after handling chillies.

1 Cut off the cap and slit open lengthways. Using a spoon, scrape out the seeds and the pith. (These are the hottest parts of the chilli.)

2 For diced chilli, cut into thin shreds lengthways, then cut crossways.

Celery

1 To remove the strings in the outer green stalks, trim the ends and cut through the base to separate the stalks. Set aside the inner ones.

2 Cut into the base of the green outer stalks with a small knife and catch the strings between the blade and your thumb. Pull up towards the top of the stalk to remove the string. Continue along the outside of the stalk.

Preparing celery, fennel, asparagus and corn

The delicate flavours of asparagus and fennel are excellent in salads, and are just as tasty eaten raw as cooked.

Fennel

1 Trim off the top stems and the base of the bulbs. Remove the core with a small sharp knife if necessary.

2 The outer leaves may be discoloured and can be scrubbed gently in cold water, or you can peel away the discoloured parts with a knife or a vegetable peeler. Slice the fennel or cut it into quarters, according to your recipe.

Asparagus

1 Cut or snap off the woody stem of each asparagus spear about 5cm (2in) from the stalk end, or where the white and green sections meet. Or cut off the stalk end and peel with a vegetable peeler or small sharp knife.

Cook's Tips

To roast asparagus, drizzle with olive oil, a few spoonfuls of water and a little salt and roast in a preheated oven, 200°C (180°C fan oven) mark 6, for 12–15 minutes, depending on the thickness of the asparagus.

To cook in water, heat a large pan of salted water that will hold the asparagus in a single layer. Put in the spears and simmer for 5 minutes until tender, then drain.

Corn on the cob

The sugar in corn starts to turn to starch soon after picking so it is best eaten as soon as possible after picking or buying. To bake, microwave or barbecue corn, leave it in its husk. To boil, you will need to remove it from its husk. Corn kernels add a crunchy sweetness to any salad.

1 **To husk** Pull away the green papery husks from the ear, a few at a time, until the whole ear is exposed.

2 Grasp the stalk and snap it off, taking all the husks with it. Rub the cob firmly with your hand to remove all the silky threads.

3 **To remove the kernels** Hold the ear upright in a large bowl, with the stalk sitting on the base of the bowl. Using a thin-bladed knife, cut off the kernels from top to bottom, turning the cob until they are all removed.

1

Preparing other vegetables

Mushrooms and garlic can be eaten either raw or cooked. The most common mushrooms are cultivated white mushrooms, but brown cap and chestnut mushrooms also add texture and flavour to salads. Raw garlic has a pungent flavour and aroma – when cooked, it is milder. For eating raw in salads, vegetables often need to be cut into small pieces or matchsticks. Ensure you have a sharp knife.

Garlic

1 Put the clove on the chopping board and put the flat side of a large knife on top of it. Press down firmly on the flat of the blade to crush the clove and break the papery skin.

2 Cut off the base of the clove and slip the garlic out of its skin. It should come away easily.

3 **Slicing** Using a rocking motion with the knife tip on the board, slice the garlic as thinly as you need.

4 **Shredding and chopping** Holding the slices together, shred them across the slices. Chop the shreds if you need chopped garlic.

5 **Crushing** After step 2, the whole clove can be put into a garlic press. To crush with a knife, roughly chop the peeled cloves and put them on the board with a pinch of salt.

6 **Puréeing** Press down hard with the edge of a large knife tip (with the blade facing away from you), then drag the blade along the garlic while still pressing hard. Continue to do this, dragging the knife tip over the garlic.

Mushrooms

Button, white, chestnut and flat mushrooms are all prepared in a similar way.

1 Wipe with a damp cloth or pastry brush to remove any dirt.

2 With button mushrooms, cut off the stalk flush with the base of the cap. For other mushrooms, cut a thin disc off the end of the stalk and discard. Chop or slice the mushrooms.

Beetroot

Young beetroot can be grated and used raw in salads. Larger beetroot should be cooked first. When preparing raw beetroot, wear rubber gloves and work over a plate rather than a chopping board, as the beetroot colour will stain your hands and the board. Be careful of your clothing, too. Wash the beetroot carefully to avoid tearing the skin, then boil for 30-40 minutes until tender. After cooking, refresh in cold water then peel, slice or dice. Look out for ready-cooked vacuum-packed beetroot, with no additives, preservatives or vinegar.

Slicing

Raw carrots and courgettes add crunch to many salads.

1 First, peel and cut off the ends. Cut slices off each of the rounded sides to make four flat surfaces that are stable on the chopping board.

2 Hold steady with one hand and cut lengthways into even slices.

Slicing with a mandolin

A mandolin makes it easy to cut uniformly thin slices or matchsticks.

1 Put the mandolin on a chopping board and set the blade to the required thickness. Push the pieces of vegetable across the blade with a swift, decisive motion, taking care to protect your fingers.

2 To make julienne (matchsticks), use either the fine or coarse julienne blade and swiftly push the pieces of vegetable across the blade.

Griddling and grilling

A few vegetables are perfect for cooking on a griddle or under the grill before being added to salads. Those that work well in both methods are courgettes and aubergines. Peppers (whole or halved) can be grilled and so can fennel, onions and sweet potatoes, with careful slicing.

Lemon and Dill Courgettes

To serve four, you will need:
450g (1lb) courgettes, cut lengthways into 5mm (¼in) slices, or quartered if small, about 6 tbsp extra virgin olive oil, ½ lemon, a small handful of fresh dill.

1 Preheat the griddle over a medium to high heat. Brush the courgettes with oil.

2 Cook the courgettes without disturbing them until they have deep brown seared lines underneath, about 2–3 minutes. Turn them and griddle until seared underneath and tender, but still with a hint of bite.

3 Remove to a plate, squeeze over lemon juice to taste and scatter with dill.

Perfect griddling

- Vegetables have a lovely flavour when cooked on the griddle, as well as attractive browned lines if you use a ridged griddle.
- The choice of vegetable is crucial in griddling: you have to use something that has a fairly even surface so that it will lie flat on the griddle and won't break up when it's turned.
- Don't slice the vegetables too thickly or they will burn before they get fully cooked – 1cm (½in) should be the maximum thickness.
- Lay the vegetables on a board and brush them with oil so that it coats them thoroughly.
- Cook over a medium-high heat and turn once, when they have browned underneath.

Washing

1 Trim the roots and part of the stalks from the herbs. Immerse in cold water and shake briskly. Leave in the water for a few minutes.

2 Lift out of the water and put in a colander or sieve, then rinse again under the cold tap. Leave to drain for a few minutes, then dry thoroughly on kitchen paper or teatowels, or use a salad spinner.

Chopping

1 Trim the herbs by pinching off all but the smallest, most tender stalks. If the herb is one with a woody stalk, such as rosemary or thyme, it may be easier to remove the leaves by rubbing the whole bunch between your hands; the leaves should simply pull off the stems.

2 If you are chopping the leaves, gather them into a compact ball in one hand, keeping your fist around the ball (but being careful not to crush them).

3 Chop with a large knife, using a rocking motion and letting just a little of the ball out of your fingers at a time.

4 When the herbs are roughly chopped, continue chopping until the pieces are in small shreds or flakes.

Using herbs

Most herbs are the leaf of a flowering plant, and are usually sold with much of the stalk intact. They have to be washed, trimmed and then chopped or torn into pieces suitable for your recipe.

Perfect herbs

- Don't pour the herbs and their water into the sieve, because dirt in the water might get caught in the leaves.
- If the herb has fleshy stalks, such as parsley or coriander, the stalks can be saved to flavour stock or soup. Tie them in a bundle with string for easy removal.

1

Preparing fruits

Citrus, stone, exotic and soft fruits, as well as berries, can all be used to give colour and flavour to salads.

Stripping currants

Blackcurrants, redcurrants and whitecurrants can all be stripped quickly and simply from the stem in the same way.

1 Using a fork, strip all the currants off the stalks by running the fork down the length of each stalk.

2 Put the currants into a colander and wash them gently, then dry on kitchen paper.

Citrus fruits

Citrus zest is an important flavouring and is simple to prepare. Segments or slices of citrus used in recipes need to be prepared so that no skin, pith or membrane remains.

Zesting

1 Wash and thoroughly dry the fruit. Using a zester, grater or vegetable peeler, cut away the zest (the coloured outer layer of skin), taking care to leave behind the bitter white pith. Continue until you have removed as much as you need.

2 Stack the slices of zest on a board and, using a sharp knife, shred or dice as required.

Segmenting

1 Cut off a slice at both ends of the fruit, then cut off the peel, just inside the white pith.

2 Hold the fruit over a bowl to catch the juice and cut between the segments just inside the membrane to release the flesh. Continue until all the segments are removed. Squeeze the juice from the membrane into the bowl and use as required.

Easy zesting

- To use a zester, press the blade into the citrus skin and run it along the surface to take off long shreds.
- To use a grater, rub the fruit over the grater, using a medium pressure to remove the zest without removing the white pith.

Stoning larger fruits

Peaches, nectarines, plums, greengages and apricots can all be handled in the same way.

1 Following the cleft along one side of the fruit, cut through to the stone all around the fruit.

2 Twist gently to separate the halves. Ease out the stone with a small knife. Rub the flesh with lemon juice.

Peeling peaches

1 Peaches may be peeled for use in salads and desserts. Put them into a bowl of boiling water for 15–60 seconds (depending on ripeness). Don't leave in the water for too long, as heat will soften the flesh. Transfer them to a bowl of cold water.

2 Work a knife between the skin and flesh to loosen the skin, then gently pull to remove. Rub the flesh with lemon juice.

Papaya

To use papaya in a salad, peel the fruit first, using a swivel-headed vegetable peeler. Then, using a sharp knife, halve the fruit lengthways and use a teaspoon to scoop out the shiny black seeds and fibres. Slice the flesh, or cut into cubes as required.

Melons

1 Halve the melon by cutting horizontally through the middle.

2 Use a spoon to scoop out the seeds and fibres, and pull or cut out any that remain.

3 **Balling** Cut into the flesh close to the hollow left by the seeds with a melon baller to scoop out a ball. Continue along the perimeter of the hollow until you have come full circle. Keep scooping until you have scooped out all of the soft flesh. (Avoid the harder flesh just under the skin.)

4 **Slicing** Cut each seeded half into slices of the required thickness. Trim off the skin in a single piece, taking care to remove the harder flesh just inside it (the knife will meet more resistance here than when it meets the softer flesh).

Preparing long-grain rice

Long-grain rice needs no special preparation, though basmati should be washed to remove excess starch.

1 Put in a bowl and cover with cold water. Stir until this becomes cloudy, then drain and repeat the washing process until the water is clear.

2 Soak the rice for 30 minutes, then drain before cooking.

Cooking rice, other grains and pasta

There are two main types of rice: long-grain and short-grain. Short-grain rice is used for dishes such as risotto, sushi and paella. Long-grain rice is generally used as an accompaniment or in salads. With any grain, the cooking time depends on how the grain has been processed. Cooked couscous, bulgur wheat and quinoa are all great in salads, as is pasta.

Cooking long-grain rice

1 Measure the rice by volume and put it in a pan with a pinch of salt with twice the volume of boiling water (or boiling stock).

2 Bring to the boil. Turn the heat down to low, and set the timer for the time stated on the pack. It needs to cook al dente: tender but with a hint of bite at the centre.

3 When the rice is cooked, fluff up the grains by gently tossing with a fork; this keeps the grains from sticking together. For using in salads, toss with a little salad dressing of your choice and leave to cool.

Perfect rice

- Use 50–75g (2–3oz) raw rice per person – or measure by volume 50–75ml (2–2½fl oz).
- If you often cook rice, you may want to invest in a special rice steamer. They are available in Asian supermarkets and some kitchen shops and give good, consistent results.

Couscous

Often mistaken for a grain, couscous is actually a type of pasta that originated in North Africa. It is perfect for making into salads or serving with stews and casseroles. The tiny pellets do not require cooking and can simply be soaked.

1 Measure the couscous in a jug and add 1½ times the volume of hot water or stock.

2 Cover the bowl and leave to soak for 5 minutes. Fluff up with a fork before serving.

3 If using for a salad, leave the couscous to cool completely before adding the other salad ingredients.

Bulgur wheat

A form of cracked wheat, bulgur has had some or all of the bran removed. It is good used in salads or served as a grain. It is pre-boiled during manufacturing and may be boiled, steamed or soaked.

Simmering Place the bulgur in a pan and cover with water by about 2.5cm (1in). Bring to the boil, then simmer for 10–15 minutes until just tender. Drain well.

Steaming Line a steamer with a clean teatowel, place the bulgur in the steamer and steam over boiling water for 20 minutes or until the grains are soft.

Soaking Put the bulgur in a deep bowl. Cover with hot water and mix with a fork. Leave to steep for 20 minutes, checking to make sure there is enough water. Drain and fluff up with a fork.

Quinoa

This nutritious South American grain makes a great alternative to rice.

1 Put the quinoa in a bowl of cold water. Mix well, soak for 2 minutes and drain. Put in a pan with twice its volume of water. Bring to the boil.

2 Simmer for 20 minutes. Remove from the heat, cover and leave to stand for 10 minutes.

Cooking pasta

This simple task has attracted a number of mistaken ideas, such as adding oil to the water, rinsing the pasta after cooking and adding salt only at a certain point. The basics couldn't be simpler.

Cooking dried pasta

1 Heat the water with about 1 tsp salt per 100g (3½oz) of pasta. Cover the pan to speed up boiling.

2 When the water has reached a rolling boil, put in all the pasta.

3 Stir well for 30 seconds, to keep the pasta from sticking either to itself or the pan. Once boiling, set the timer for 2 minutes less than the recommended cooking time on the pack and cook uncovered.

4 Check the pasta when the timer goes off, then every 60 seconds until it is cooked al dente: tender with a little bite at the centre. Scoop out a cup of cooking water (it may be useful for loosening up a thick sauce).

5 Drain the pasta well in a colander. Transfer to a serving bowl, and use as required by your recipe.

Cooking fresh pasta

Fresh pasta is cooked in the same way as dried, but for a shorter time.

1 Bring the water to the boil.

2 Add the pasta to the boiling water and stir well. Set the timer for 2 minutes and keep testing every 30 seconds until the pasta is cooked al dente: tender but with a little bite in the centre. Drain as above.

Perfect pasta

- Use about 1 litre (1¾ pints) of water per 100g (3½oz) of pasta.
- Rinse the pasta only if you are going to cool it for use in a salad, then drain well and toss with oil.
- If a recipe calls for cooking the pasta with the sauce after it has boiled, undercook the pasta slightly when boiling it.

Herb Vinegar

To make 600ml (1 pint), you will need:
25g (1oz) fresh herbs, plus extra sprigs for bottling, 600ml (1 pint) red or white wine vinegar.

1 Put the herbs and vinegar in a pan and bring to the boil. Pour into a bowl, cover and leave overnight.

2 Strain through a muslin-lined sieve and bottle with herb sprigs. Store for one week before using.

Fruit Vinegar

To make 600ml (1 pint), you will need:
450g (1lb) raspberries and blackberries, plus extra for bottling, 600ml (1 pint) red wine vinegar.

1 Break up the fruit with the back of a spoon and add the vinegar. Cover and leave to stand 3 days, stirring now and then.

2 Strain through a muslin-lined sieve and bottle with extra fruits. Store for two weeks before using.

Making flavoured vinegars

These are easy to make using tarragon, thyme or rosemary, and can be stored in a cool dark place for one month. Use sterilised storage bottles, wash all the ingredients well and dry before adding to the vinegar.

Making salad dressings

Whether you prefer your dressing tart and piquant or rich and creamy, always dress and toss your salad just before serving, and avoid overdressing – instead simply aim to coat the leaves well.

Balsamic Dressing

To make about 100ml (3½fl oz), you will need:
2 tbsp balsamic vinegar, 4 tbsp extra virgin olive oil, salt and ground black pepper.

1 Whisk the vinegar and oil in a small bowl. Season with salt and pepper to taste.

2 If not using immediately, store in a cool place and whisk briefly before using.

Cook's Tips

To help it emulsify easily, add 1 tsp cold water to the dressing.
To get a really good emulsion, shake the dressing vigorously in a screw-topped jar.

French Dressing

To make 100ml (3½fl oz), you will need:
1 tsp Dijon mustard, a pinch of sugar, 1 tbsp red or white wine vinegar, 6 tbsp extra virgin olive oil, salt and ground black pepper.

1 Put the mustard, sugar and vinegar in a small bowl, and season with salt and pepper.

2 Whisk thoroughly until well combined, then gradually whisk in the oil until thoroughly combined. If not using immediately, store in a cool place and whisk briefly before using.

French Dressing variations

Herb Dressing Use half the mustard, replace the vinegar with lemon juice, and add 2 tbsp freshly chopped herbs, such as parsley, chervil and chives.
Garlic Dressing Add 1 crushed garlic clove to the dressing at step 2.

Twelve quick salad dressings

Basic Vinaigrette

To make about 300ml (½ pint) you will need:
100ml (3½fl oz) extra virgin olive oil, 100ml (3½fl oz) grapeseed oil, 50ml (2fl oz) white wine vinegar, a pinch each of sugar and English mustard powder, 1 garlic clove, crushed (optional), salt and ground black pepper.

1 Put both oils, the vinegar, sugar, mustard powder and garlic, if using, into a large screw-topped jar. Tighten the lid and shake well. Season to taste with salt and pepper.

2 If not using immediately, store in a cool place and shake briefly before using.

Lemon Vinaigrette

To make about 150ml (¼ pint) you will need:
2 tbsp lemon juice, 2 tsp runny honey, 8 tbsp extra virgin olive oil, 3 tbsp freshly chopped mint, 4 tbsp roughly chopped flat-leafed parsley, salt and ground black pepper.

1 Put the lemon juice, honey and salt and pepper to taste in a small bowl and whisk to combine.

2 Gradually whisk in the olive oil and stir in the chopped herbs. If not using immediately, store in a cool place and whisk briefly before using.

Mustard

To make about 100ml (3½fl oz) you will need:
1 tbsp wholegrain mustard, juice of ½ lemon, 6 tbsp extra virgin olive oil, salt and ground black pepper.

1 Put the mustard, lemon juice and olive oil in a small bowl and whisk together. Season to taste with salt and pepper.

2 If not using immediately, store in a cool place and whisk briefly before using.

Lemon and Parsley

To make about 100ml (3½fl oz), you will need:
juice of ½ lemon, 6 tbsp extra virgin olive oil, 4 tbsp freshly chopped flat-leafed parsley, salt and ground black pepper.

1 Put the lemon juice, olive oil and parsley in a medium bowl and whisk together. Season to taste with salt and pepper.

2 If not using immediately, store in a cool place and whisk briefly before using.

Blue Cheese

To make 100ml (3½fl oz), you will need:
50g (2oz) Roquefort cheese, 2 tbsp low-fat yogurt, 1 tbsp white wine vinegar, 5 tbsp extra virgin olive oil.

1 Crumble the cheese into a food processor with the yogurt, vinegar and olive oil.

2 Whiz for 1 minute until thoroughly combined. Season to taste with salt and pepper. Store in a cool place and use within 1 day.

Chilli Lime

To make 125ml (4fl oz), you will need:
¼ red chilli, seeded and finely chopped, 1 garlic clove, crushed, 1cm (½in) piece fresh root ginger, peeled and finely grated, juice of 1½ large limes, 50ml (2fl oz) olive oil, 1½ tbsp light muscovado sugar, 2 tbsp coriander leaves, 2 tbsp mint leaves.

1 Put the chilli, garlic, ginger, lime juice, olive oil and sugar into a food processor or blender and whiz for 10 seconds to combine.

2 Add the coriander and mint and whiz together for 5 seconds to chop roughly. Store in a cool place and use within two days.

Garlic, Soy and Honey

To make about 100ml (3½fl oz), you will need:
1 garlic clove, crushed, 2 tsp each soy sauce and honey,
1 tbsp cider vinegar, 4 tbsp olive oil, ground black pepper.

1 Put the garlic in a small bowl. Add the soy sauce,
honey, vinegar and olive oil, season to taste with
pepper and whisk together thoroughly.

2 If not using immediately, store in a cool place and
whisk briefly before using.

Mint Yogurt

To make about 175ml (6fl oz), you will need:
150g (5oz) Greek yogurt, 3–4 tbsp chopped mint leaves,
2 tbsp extra virgin olive oil, salt and ground black pepper.

1 Put the yogurt in a bowl and add the mint and
olive oil. Season to taste with salt and pepper.

2 If not using immediately, store in a cool place and
use within one day.

Sun-dried Tomato

To make about 100ml (3½fl oz), you will need:
2 sun-dried tomatoes in oil, drained, 2 tbsp oil from
sun-dried tomato jar, 2 tbsp red wine vinegar, 1 garlic
clove, 1 tbsp sun-dried tomato paste, a pinch of sugar
(optional), 2 tbsp extra virgin olive oil, salt and ground
black pepper.

1 Put the sun-dried tomatoes and oil, the vinegar,
garlic and tomato paste into a blender or food
processor. Add the sugar, if using.

2 With the motor running, pour the olive oil through
the feeder tube and whiz briefly to make a fairly
thick dressing. Season to taste with salt and pepper.
If not using immediately, store in a cool place and
whisk briefly before using.

Classic Coleslaw

To make about 175ml (6fl oz), you will need:
2½ tbsp red wine vinegar, 125ml (4fl oz) olive oil, 1 tbsp
Dijon mustard, salt and ground black pepper.

1 Pour the vinegar into a large screw-topped jar. Add
the olive oil and mustard and season with salt and
pepper. Screw on the lid and shake well.

2 Combine with the coleslaw ingredients and chill
until needed.

Chilli Coleslaw

To make about 100ml (3½fl oz), you will need:
½ tsp harissa, 100g (3½oz) natural yogurt, 1 tbsp white
wine vinegar.

1 Put all the ingredients into a small bowl and whisk
to combine.

2 Combine with the coleslaw ingredients and chill
until needed.

Caesar

To make about 150ml (¼ pint), you will need:
1 medium egg, 1 garlic clove, juice of ½ lemon, 2 tsp
Dijon mustard, 1 tsp balsamic vinegar, 150ml (¼ pint)
sunflower oil, salt and ground black pepper.

1 Put the eggs garlic, lemon juice, mustard and
vinegar in a food processor and whiz until smooth
then, with the motor running, gradually add the oil
and whiz until smooth.

2 Season with salt and pepper, cover and chill for up
to three days.

Making mayonnaise

The simplest of accompaniments, mayonnaise goes well with salads, poached fish and poultry. For salads, you can flavour the basic mayonnaise with a variety of herbs, vegetables and fruit.

Mayonnaise

To make about 250ml (9fl oz), you will need:
2 large egg yolks, 1 tsp English mustard, 200ml (7fl oz) sunflower oil, 100ml (3½fl oz) virgin olive oil, 1 tsp white wine vinegar or lemon juice, salt and ground black pepper.

1 Put the egg yolks in a 900ml (1½ pint) bowl. Stir in the mustard, 1 tsp salt and plenty of black pepper.

2 Combine the oils and add 1 tsp to the egg yolks. Whisk thoroughly, then add another 1 tsp and whisk until thickened. Continue adding about half the oil, 1 tbsp at a time. Whisk in the vinegar or lemon juice, then add the oil in a thin, steady stream until the mayonnaise is thick.

3 Check the seasoning, adding more vinegar or lemon juice if necessary. Cover and chill for up to four days.

Cook's Tips

Sometimes mayonnaise splits or curdles but it's easy to fix:
- Add a splash of cold water (about 1 tbsp) and stir in with a spoon. Continue with the recipe.
- If this doesn't work, put another egg yolk into a clean bowl and gradually whisk in the curdled mixture 1 tbsp at a time.

Mayonnaise variations

Lemon and Garlic

To make about 150ml (¼ pint), you will need:
175ml (6fl oz) mayonnaise, 1 tbsp grated lemon zest,
plus 1 tbsp lemon juice, 2 finely chopped spring
onions, 1 garlic clove, crushed, salt and ground
black pepper.

1 Put all the ingredients into a medium bowl and
beat well to combine. Check the seasoning.

2 Cover and chill for up to two days.

Smoky Pepper

To make about 175ml (6fl oz), you will need:
1 grilled red pepper, peeled and chopped, 1 garlic
clove, 250ml (9fl oz) mayonnaise, 2 tsp chilli oil,
2 tbsp lemon juice.

1 Put the red pepper, garlic and mayonnaise in a
processor and whiz to combine.

2 Stir in the chilli oil and lemon juice. Cover and
chill for up to two days.

Mango

To make about 175ml (6fl oz), you will need:
1 large mango, peeled and stoned, 2 tsp freshly
chopped coriander, 1 tsp peeled and grated fresh root
ginger, juice of 1 lime, 200ml (7fl oz) sunflower oil,
salt and ground black pepper.

1 Mash the flesh of the mango in a bowl and add
the coriander, ginger and lime juice. Season well
with salt and pepper.

2 Slowly whisk in the oil until the mayonnaise is
thick. Cover and chill for up to two days.

Separating eggs

This simple technique will come in handy for a great many
recipes. It's easy, but it requires some care.

1 Crack the egg more carefully than usual: right in the
middle to make a break between the two halves that
is just wide enough to get your thumbnail into.

2 Holding the egg over a bowl with the large end
pointing down, carefully lift off the small half. Some
of the white will drip and slide into the bowl while
the yolk sits in the large end of the shell.

3 Carefully slide the yolk into the smaller end, then
back into the large end to allow the remaining white
to drop into the bowl. Take care not to break the yolk:
even a speck can stop the whites from whisking up.

Cook's Tip

If you're separating more than one egg, break each one
into an individual cup. Separating them individually means
that if you break one yolk, you won't spoil the whole batch.

Food storage and hygiene

Storing food properly and preparing it in a hygienic way is important to ensure that food remains as nutritious and flavourful as possible, and to reduce the risk of food poisoning.

Hygiene

When you are preparing food, always follow these important guidelines:

Wash your hands thoroughly before handling food and again between handling different types of food, such as raw and cooked meat and poultry. If you have any cuts or grazes on your hands, be sure to keep them covered with a waterproof plaster.

Wash down worksurfaces regularly with a mild detergent solution or multi-surface cleaner.

Use a dishwasher if available. Otherwise, wear rubber gloves for washing-up, so that the water temperature can be hotter than unprotected hands can bear. Change drying-up cloths and cleaning cloths regularly. Note that leaving dishes to drain is more hygienic than drying them with a teatowel.

Keep raw and cooked foods separate, especially meat, fish and poultry. Wash kitchen utensils in between preparing raw and cooked foods. Never put cooked or ready-to-eat foods directly on to a surface which has just had raw fish, meat or poultry on it.

Keep pets out of the kitchen if possible; or make sure they stay away from worksurfaces. Never allow animals on to worksurfaces.

Shopping

Always choose fresh ingredients in prime condition from stores and markets that have a regular turnover of stock to ensure you buy the freshest produce possible.

Make sure items are within their 'best before' or 'use by' date. (Foods with a longer shelf life have a 'best before' date; more perishable items have a 'use by' date.)

Pack frozen and chilled items in an insulated cool bag at the check-out and put them into the freezer or refrigerator as soon as you get home.

During warm weather in particular, buy perishable foods just before you return home. When packing items at the check-out, sort them according to where you will store them when you get home – the refrigerator, freezer, storecupboard, vegetable rack, fruit bowl, etc. This will make unpacking easier – and quicker.

The storecupboard

Although storecupboard ingredients will generally last a long time, correct storage is important:

Always check packaging for storage advice – even with familiar foods, because storage requirements may change if additives, sugar or salt have been reduced. Check storecupboard foods for their 'best before' or 'use by' date and do not use them if the date has passed.

Keep all food cupboards scrupulously clean and make sure food containers and packets are properly sealed.

Once opened, treat canned foods as though fresh. Always transfer the contents to a clean container, cover and keep in the refrigerator. Similarly, jars, sauce bottles and cartons should be kept chilled after opening. (Check the label for safe storage times after opening.)

Transfer dry goods such as sugar, rice and pasta to moisture-proof containers. When supplies are used up, wash the container well and thoroughly dry before refilling with new supplies.

Store oils in a dark cupboard away from any heat source as heat and light can make them turn rancid and affect their colour. For the same reason, buy olive oil in dark green bottles.

Store vinegars in a cool place; they can turn bad in a warm environment.

Store dried herbs, spices and flavourings in a cool, dark cupboard or in dark jars. Buy in small quantities as their flavour will not last indefinitely.

Store flours and sugars in airtight containers.

Refrigerator storage

Fresh food needs to be stored in the cool temperature of the refrigerator to keep it in good condition and discourage the growth of harmful bacteria. Store day-to-day perishable items, such as opened jams and jellies, mayonnaise and bottled sauces, in the refrigerator along with eggs and dairy products, fruit juices, bacon, fresh and cooked meat (on separate shelves), and salads and vegetables (except potatoes, which don't suit being stored in the cold). A refrigerator should be kept at an operating temperature of 4–5°C. It is worth investing in a refrigerator thermometer to ensure the correct temperature is maintained.

To ensure your refrigerator is functioning effectively for safe food storage, follow these guidelines:

To avoid bacterial cross-contamination, store cooked and raw foods on separate shelves, putting cooked foods on the top shelf. Ensure that all items are well wrapped.

Never put hot food into the refrigerator, as this will cause the internal temperature of the refrigerator to rise.

Avoid overfilling the refrigerator, as this restricts the circulation of air and prevents the appliance from working properly.

It can take some time for the refrigerator to return to the correct operating temperature once the door has been opened, so don't leave it open any longer than is necessary.

Clean the refrigerator regularly, using a specially formulated germicidal refrigerator cleaner. Alternatively, use a weak solution of bicarbonate of soda: 1 tbsp to 1 litre (1¾ pints) water.

If your refrigerator doesn't have an automatic defrost facility, defrost regularly.

Maximum refrigerator storage times

For pre-packed foods, always adhere to the 'use by' date on the packet. For other foods the following storage times should apply, providing the food is in prime condition when it goes into the refrigerator and that your refrigerator is in good working order:

Vegetables and Fruit

Green vegetables	3–4 days
Salad leaves	2–3 days
Hard and stone fruit	3–7 days
Soft fruit	1–2 days

Dairy Food

Cheese, hard	1 week
Cheese, soft	2–3 days
Eggs	1 week
Milk	4–5 days

Fish

Fish	1 day
Shellfish	1 day

Raw Meat

Bacon	7 days
Game	2 days
Offal	1 day
Poultry	2 days
Raw sliced meat	2 days

Cooked Meat

Pies	2 days
Sliced meat	2 days
Ham	2 days
Ham, vacuum-packed (or according to the instructions on the packet)	1–2 weeks

Starters

Pear, Grape and Parmesan Salad

125g (4oz) white seedless grapes, halved

2 large ripe pears, peeled, cored and thickly sliced

150g (5oz) rocket

175g (6oz) Parmesan, pared into shavings with a vegetable peeler

50g (2oz) walnut pieces

For the dressing

1 tbsp white wine vinegar

1/2 tsp Dijon mustard

3 tbsp walnut oil

1 tbsp sunflower oil

salt and ground black pepper

1 Whisk all the dressing ingredients together in a small bowl and season with salt and pepper.

2 Put the grapes and pears into a bowl, pour the dressing over and toss together. Leave to marinate for 15 minutes.

3 Just before serving, tear the rocket into smallish pieces, put in a large bowl, add the grape and pear mixture and toss together. Divide the salad among four serving plates and serve topped with the Parmesan shavings and the walnut pieces.

Try Something Different

Apple, Celery and Hazelnut Salad: replace the walnut oil with hazelnut oil, the grapes with 2 sliced celery sticks, the pears with apples and the walnuts with toasted, roughly chopped hazelnuts.

Serves 4	EASY	NUTRITIONAL INFORMATION	
	Preparation Time 15 minutes, plus 15 minutes marinating	Per Serving 440 calories, 34g fat (of which 11g saturates), 13g carbohydrate, 1.3g salt	Vegetarian Gluten free

Avocado, Clementine and Chicory Salad

4 chicory heads, leaves separated

3 clementines or satsumas, peeled and thinly sliced into rounds

2 ripe avocados, halved, stoned, peeled and sliced

25g (1oz) pinenuts, toasted

For the orange and dill dressing

juice of ½ orange

4 tbsp olive oil

2 tbsp finely chopped fresh dill

salt and ground black pepper

1 To make the dressing, put the orange juice into a small bowl and add the olive oil and dill. Season with salt and pepper and whisk everything together.

2 Scatter the chicory on a serving plate and arrange the clementines or satsumas and avocados on top. Sprinkle over the pinenuts and spoon the dressing over the salad.

Serves 6	EASY	NUTRITIONAL INFORMATION	
	Preparation Time 10 minutes	**Per Serving** 187 calories, 19g fat (of which 3g saturates), 4g carbohydrate, trace salt	Vegetarian Gluten free • Dairy free

a selection of bitter leaves, such as curly endive, radicchio and chicory

225g (8oz) Roquefort cheese, crumbled

125g (4oz) fresh redcurrants – reserve four sprays to garnish and destalk the rest

Roquefort and Redcurrant Salad

For the dressing

1½ tbsp redcurrant jelly

1 tbsp white wine vinegar

a pinch of English mustard powder

4 tbsp extra virgin olive oil

salt and ground black pepper

1 To make the dressing, put the redcurrant jelly, 1 tsp boiling water, the vinegar, mustard powder and olive oil into a small bowl and whisk until combined. Season with salt and pepper.

2 Arrange the salad leaves and Roquefort on a large plate. Spoon the dressing over the top and sprinkle with the redcurrants. Garnish with redcurrant sprays and serve immediately.

EASY	NUTRITIONAL INFORMATION		Serves
Preparation Time 10 minutes	**Per Serving** 320 calories, 27g fat (of which 12g saturates), 7g carbohydrate, 1.7g salt	Vegetarian Gluten free	4

Gravadlax with Cucumber Salad

1 small cucumber, halved lengthways, seeded and thinly sliced

3 tbsp white wine vinegar

1 tbsp caster sugar

3 tbsp freshly chopped dill

2 x 125g packs gravadlax with dill and mustard sauce

4 tbsp crème fraîche

12 mini blinis

salt and ground black pepper

fresh dill sprigs to garnish

1 Arrange the cucumber on a large plate. Mix the vinegar with the caster sugar and chopped dill, then season to taste with salt and pepper. Pour the dressing over the cucumber and leave to marinate for 15 minutes.

2 Mix the dill and mustard sauce into the crème fraîche and season with salt and pepper.

3 Lightly toast the blinis. Arrange the marinated cucumber on four serving plates with the slices of gravadlax, the crème fraîche sauce and the blinis. Garnish with dill sprigs to serve.

EASY		NUTRITIONAL INFORMATION	Serves
Preparation Time 15 minutes, plus 15 minutes marinating	**Cooking Time** 2–3 minutes	**Per Serving** 316 calories, 19g fat (of which 5g saturates), 16g carbohydrate, 3.2g salt	**4**

Cook's Tip

Sunblush tomatoes are dried in the sun to preserve them and concentrate the flavours in the same way as sun-dried tomatoes, but are not as dehydrated as sun-dried tomatoes.

Peppers with Rocket and Balsamic Salsa

4 red peppers, halved and seeded, each half cut lengthways into three

4 tbsp olive oil

2 garlic cloves, sliced

1 small red onion, chopped

8 fresh thyme sprigs

2 tbsp balsamic vinegar

125g (4oz) sunblush tomatoes (see Cook's Tip)

100g (3½oz) wild rocket

salt and ground black pepper

1 Preheat the oven to 220°C (200°C fan oven) mark 7. Put the peppers into a roasting tin, then drizzle with 1½ tbsp olive oil and roast for 30 minutes until tender and slightly charred. After 15 minutes, add the garlic, chopped onion and thyme to the tin and drizzle with 1 tbsp olive oil. Roast for a further 15 minutes.

2 To make the balsamic salsa, pick the roasted thyme leaves from the stalks (discarding the stalks) and put into a small screw-topped jar with the roasted onion and garlic. Add 1½ tbsp olive oil and the balsamic vinegar, then drain off any oil from the sunblush tomatoes and add this, too. Season generously with salt and pepper, screw on the lid and shake well to combine.

3 Put the peppers on four serving plates, put the rocket on top, then scatter the sunblush tomatoes over. Drizzle with the balsamic salsa at the last minute.

Serves 4	EASY		NUTRITIONAL INFORMATION	
	Preparation Time 15 minutes	**Cooking Time** 30 minutes	**Per Serving** 177 calories, 12g fat (of which 2g saturates), 15g carbohydrate, 0.2g salt	Vegetarian Gluten free • Dairy free

Try Something Different

Include other ingredients in this Italian-inspired salad, according to what's available: try quartered fresh figs, slices of melon, Parma ham or salami, buffalo mozzarella or marinated grilled artichokes.

Antipasto Salad

juice of 1 lime

4 ripe pears, peaches or nectarines, halved, stoned and sliced

50g (2oz) rocket

4–5 small firm round goat's cheeses, thickly sliced

4 grilled red peppers, sliced, or a 285g jar pimientos, drained

2 small red onions, sliced into petals

a handful of black olives

olive oil to drizzle

ground black pepper

1 Squeeze the lime juice over the fruit and add a sprinkling of black pepper.

2 Arrange all the ingredients on six serving plates.

3 Cover with clingfilm and keep in a cool place. Use within 2 hours. Drizzle with olive oil just before serving.

EASY	NUTRITIONAL INFORMATION		Serves
Preparation Time 15 minutes	**Per Serving** 129 calories, 6g fat (of which 3g saturates), 15g carbohydrate, 0.8g salt	Vegetarian Gluten free	**6**

Cook's Tip

If you can't find baby mozzarella, buy larger buffalo mozzarella instead – available from most major supermarkets – and cut it into large cubes.

Tomato, Mozzarella and Red Pesto Salad

225g (8oz) baby plum tomatoes, halved

225g (8oz) baby mozzarella, drained (see Cook's Tip)

100g jar red pepper pesto

175g (6oz) pitted black olives, drained

100g (3½oz) mixed salad leaves

salt and ground black pepper

fresh basil sprigs to garnish

1   Put the plum tomatoes, mozzarella, pesto and olives in a large bowl and toss together. Season with pepper and, if necessary, add salt – the olives are already salty. Cover the bowl and put to one side.

2   Just before serving the salad, toss the mixed leaves with the tomato mixture and garnish with basil sprigs.

Serves 4	EASY	NUTRITIONAL INFORMATION	
	Preparation Time 10 minutes	**Per Serving** 400 calories, 36g fat (of which 12g saturates), 3g carbohydrate, 2.9g salt	Vegetarian Gluten free

75g (3oz) pinenuts
300g (11oz) asparagus tips, trimmed
450g (1lb) chicken livers
25g (1oz) butter
125g (4oz) wild rocket

For the orange and raisin dressing
6 small oranges
200ml (7fl oz) light olive oil
4 tbsp red wine vinegar
2 tbsp clear honey
50g (2oz) raisins
salt and ground black pepper

Warm Chicken Liver Salad

1 To make the dressing, grate the zest from 2 oranges, squeeze the juice and set aside. Peel and segment the remaining 4 oranges. Pour the olive oil and vinegar into a small pan. Add 6 tbsp of the orange juice (reserving the rest), the zest, honey and raisins. Season well with salt and pepper and whisk together. Bring gently to the boil, remove from the heat and set aside.

2 Put the pinenuts in a frying pan and heat gently to toast. Tip into a bowl to cool. Cook the asparagus for 5 minutes in simmering salted water. Drain, then dry on kitchen paper.

3 Cut off any sinew and fat from the livers, then pat dry on kitchen paper. Heat the butter in a large heavy-based pan and, when the foaming has subsided, add the livers and cook over a high heat for about 5 minutes or until well browned. Remove from the pan and keep warm.

4 Add the remaining orange juice and the dressing to the pan. Allow to bubble for 1–2 minutes, stirring and scraping the pan to dissolve any meat goodness.

5 Divide the livers, orange segments, asparagus and rocket among six bowls. Scatter the pinenuts on top, spoon the dressing over and finish with a grinding of black pepper. Serve at once.

EASY		NUTRITIONAL INFORMATION		Serves
Preparation Time 10 minutes	**Cooking Time** 15–20 minutes	**Per Serving** 478 calories, 39g fat (of which 7g saturates), 14g carbohydrate, 0.3g salt	Gluten free	**6**

Melon, Mint and Crispy Ham

150g (5oz) thinly sliced Serrano or Parma ham

1½ ripe Charentais melons (see Cook's Tips)

3 spring onions, finely sliced and soaked in iced water

1 tsp mixed peppercorns, crushed

50g (2oz) Manchego (see Cook's Tips) or Parmesan, pared into shavings with a vegetable peeler

fresh mint sprigs to garnish

For the mint dressing

3–4 tbsp red wine vinegar

½ tsp caster sugar

3 tbsp freshly chopped mint

9 tbsp olive oil

a pinch of salt

1 To make the mint dressing, whisk together the vinegar, sugar, chopped mint, salt and olive oil. Put to one side.

2 Preheat the grill. Grill half the ham for 1–2 minutes until crisp, then set aside. Grill the remaining slices, then set aside to cool. Break into large pieces.

3 Quarter the whole melon, then cut the melon half into two (you should end up with six pieces). Remove the melon skin, cut the melon into chunks and divide among six plates. Top with the ham.

4 To serve, whisk the dressing again and drizzle over the melon. Top with the spring onions, then sprinkle with the crushed peppercorns and cheese shavings and garnish with mint sprigs.

Cook's Tips

When buying melons check for ripeness by pressing firmly around the stalk end – a ripe melon should give slightly when pressed.
Manchego cheese is a hard, tangy sheep's milk cheese made in the La Mancha region of Spain.
Serrano ham is Spanish cured ham, made in the same way as Parma ham.

Serves 6	EASY		NUTRITIONAL INFORMATION	
	Preparation Time 20 minutes	Cooking Time 4 minutes	Per Serving 277 calories, 20g fat (of which 4g saturates), 15g carbohydrate, 1.2g salt	Gluten free

Try Something Different

Mango, Crab and Lime Salad: replace the watermelon and papaya with 2 small ripe mangoes, peeled, stoned and sliced. Use cooked white crabmeat instead of the prawns.

Melon and Prawn Salad

1 ripe Charentais melon
½ small ripe Galia melon
1 wedge watermelon
1 papaya (optional)
grated zest and juice of 1 lime, plus extra lime zest to garnish
200ml (7fl oz) thick mayonnaise
225g (8oz) large cooked peeled prawns
salt and ground black pepper
freshly chopped coriander to garnish

1 Thickly slice the melons and remove the skin. Scoop out the seeds and strain them, reserving the juice. Cut the melons into bite-size pieces, then cover and chill. Thickly slice the papaya, if using, removing the seeds if you like, then chill.

2 Stir the lime zest and 2 tbsp each lime and melon juice into the mayonnaise and season with salt and pepper. Mix the mayonnaise and prawns together.

3 Arrange the chilled melon and papaya on four serving plates. Add the prawns and garnish with extra lime zest and chopped coriander.

Serves 4	EASY		NUTRITIONAL INFORMATION	
	Preparation Time 25 minutes, plus chilling		**Per Serving** 571 calories, 39g fat (of which 6g saturates), 44g carbohydrate, 1.1g salt	Gluten free • Dairy free

Mangetout, Avocado and Grapefruit

350g (12oz) mangetouts

1 avocado, halved, stoned, peeled and sliced

6 tbsp Basic Vinaigrette (see page 24)

1 pink grapefruit, segmented

rocket or watercress to serve

1 Blanch the mangetouts in boiling salted water for 1 minute. Drain, refresh and drain again.

2 Mix the mangetouts with the avocado, vinaigrette and grapefruit. Serve on a bed of rocket or watercress.

EASY		NUTRITIONAL INFORMATION		Serves
Preparation Time 10 minutes	**Cooking Time** 1 minute	**Per Serving** 257 calories, 19g fat (of which 4g saturates), 7g carbohydrate, 0.5g salt	Vegetarian Gluten free • Dairy free	**4**

Simple Sides

Warm Broad Bean and Feta Salad

225g (8oz) broad beans – if using fresh beans you will need to start with 700g (1½lb) pods

100g (3½oz) feta cheese, chopped

2 tbsp freshly chopped mint

2 tbsp extra virgin olive oil

a squeeze of lemon juice

salt and ground black pepper

lemon wedges to serve

1 Cook the beans in salted boiling water for 3–5 minutes until tender. Drain, then plunge into cold water and drain again.

2 Tip the beans into a bowl, add the feta, mint, olive oil and a squeeze of lemon juice. Season well with salt and pepper and toss together. Serve with lemon wedges.

Serves 2	EASY		NUTRITIONAL INFORMATION	
	Preparation Time 10 minutes	Cooking Time 5 minutes	Per Serving 321 calories, 22g fat (of which 8g saturates), 15g carbohydrate, 1.8g salt	Vegetarian Gluten free

Crisp Summer Salad

2 Romaine lettuces, leaves separated, washed, dried and cut into bite-size pieces

1 papaya, peeled, seeded and diced

1 large ripe avocado, quartered, stoned, peeled and diced

1 green pepper, seeded and finely diced

1 large white onion, finely diced

small bunch of chives

2 tbsp finely chopped flat-leafed parsley

1 tsp paprika

For the dressing

2 tbsp lemon juice

2 tbsp extra virgin olive oil

1 tbsp sweet chilli sauce

salt and ground black pepper

1 To make the dressing, mix together the lemon juice, olive oil and chilli sauce and season with salt and pepper.

2 Put the lettuce in a large bowl, add the papaya, avocado, green pepper and onion, pour the dressing over and toss well.

3 Divide the salad among four serving plates, garnish with chives and sprinkle each plate with a little parsley and paprika to serve.

EASY	NUTRITIONAL INFORMATION		Serves
Preparation Time 30 minutes	**Per Serving** 233 calories, 14g fat (of which 2g saturates), 25g carbohydrate, 0.2g salt	Vegetarian Gluten free • Dairy free	**4**

Guacamole Salad

3 beef tomatoes, each cut horizontally into six

½ small onion, finely sliced

1 garlic clove, crushed

1 tbsp fresh coriander leaves, plus extra sprigs to garnish

4 ripe avocados

juice of 1 lime

200g (7oz) feta cheese, crumbled

100g (3½oz) sunblush tomatoes in oil

salt and ground black pepper

lime wedges to serve

1 Divide the tomato slices among six serving plates, then scatter the onion, garlic and coriander over.

2 Cut each avocado into quarters as far as the stone. Keeping the avocado whole, start at the pointed end and peel away the skin. Separate each quarter, remove the stone, then slice the pieces lengthways. Squeeze the lime juice over to stop the avocado slices from browning and arrange on the plates.

3 Top with the feta cheese, sunblush tomatoes and a sprig of coriander. Finish each salad with a drizzling of oil reserved from the sunblush tomatoes and season well with salt and pepper. Serve with lime wedges.

Serves 6	EASY		NUTRITIONAL INFORMATION	
	Preparation Time 15 minutes	**Cooking Time** 20 minutes	**Per Serving** 317 calories, 28g fat (of which 9g saturates), 7g carbohydrate, 1.3g salt	Vegetarian

Try Something Different

Yogurt Dressing: mix together 5 tbsp natural yogurt with 1 tbsp each freshly chopped mint and chives and a small crushed garlic clove. Season with salt and pepper.

Tomato Dressing: halve and seed 8 cherry tomatoes and cut into thin strips. Mix 1 tbsp balsamic vinegar with 3 tbsp olive oil, 2 tbsp freshly chopped tarragon, salt and pepper. Stir in the tomato and drizzle over the vegetables.

Summer Vegetable Salad

600g (1lb 5oz) mixed green vegetables, such as green beans, peas, sugarsnap peas, trimmed asparagus, broad beans, broccoli

¼ small cucumber, halved lengthways, seeded and sliced

2 tbsp freshly chopped flat-leafed parsley

For the dressing

1 tbsp white wine vinegar or sherry vinegar

1 tsp English mustard powder

3 tbsp extra virgin olive oil

salt and ground black pepper

1 Cook the green beans in a large pan of boiling salted water for 3 minutes, then add all the other vegetables. Return the water to the boil and cook for a further 3–4 minutes. Drain and put immediately into a bowl of ice-cold water. Drain well.

2 Whisk all the dressing ingredients together in a small bowl and season with salt and pepper.

3 To serve, toss the vegetables in the dressing with the cucumber and parsley.

Serves 4	EASY		NUTRITIONAL INFORMATION	
	Preparation Time 10 minutes	**Cooking Time** 6–7 minutes	**Per Serving** 119 calories, 9g fat (of which 1g saturates), 4g carbohydrate, 0.6g salt	Vegetarian Gluten free • Dairy free

Tomato, Rocket and Parmesan Salad

150g (5oz) mixed salad leaves

50g (2oz) rocket leaves

250g (9oz) baby plum tomatoes, cut in half lengthways

50g (2oz) pinenuts, toasted

3 tbsp extra virgin olive oil

1 tbsp balsamic vinegar

75g (3oz) Parmesan, pared into shavings with a vegetable peeler

salt and ground black pepper

1 Put the salad and rocket leaves in a bowl of ice-cold water. Leave for a few minutes to crisp up, then drain through a colander and shake to remove excess water. Put in a serving bowl, add the tomatoes and pinenuts and toss well.

2 Mix together the olive oil and vinegar in a small bowl and season with salt and pepper. Pour over the salad, toss well, then scatter the Parmesan on top to serve.

EASY	NUTRITIONAL INFORMATION	Serves
Preparation Time 10–15 minutes	**Per Serving** 176 calories, 16g fat (of which 4g saturates), 2g carbohydrate, 0.4g salt	**6**

Chicory, Fennel and Orange Salad

1 small fennel bulb, with fronds

2 chicory heads or ½ head Chinese leaf, shredded

2 oranges, peeled and cut into rounds, plus juice of ½ orange

25g (1oz) hazelnuts, chopped and toasted

2 tbsp hazelnut or walnut oil

salt and ground black pepper

1 Trim the fronds from the fennel, roughly chop them and put to one side. Finely slice the fennel bulb lengthways and put in a bowl with the chicory or Chinese leaves, the orange slices and toasted hazelnuts.

2 Put the orange juice, hazelnut or walnut oil and the reserved fennel fronds in a small bowl, season well with salt and pepper and mix thoroughly. Pour over the salad and toss everything together.

EASY		NUTRITIONAL INFORMATION		Serves
Preparation Time 15 minutes	Cooking Time 2-3 minutes	Per Serving 127 calories, 10g fat (of which 1g saturates), 9g carbohydrate, trace salt	Vegetarian Gluten free • Dairy free	4

Try Something Different

Warm Pesto and Rocket Salad: omit the capers and mustard and make a dressing by mixing 4 tbsp pesto with 1 tbsp olive oil. Toss with the warm potatoes, along with a good handful of wild rocket instead of the tarragon and caperberries.

Cook's Tip

Caperberries are the fruit from the caper bush. They are larger than capers, which are the buds.

Warm New Potato Salad

650g (1lb 6oz) new potatoes, halved
1 heaped tbsp freshly chopped tarragon
caperberries to serve (see Cook's Tip)

For the caper dressing
1 heaped tbsp capers in sherry vinegar, rinsed
1 heaped tbsp Dijon mustard
4 tbsp extra virgin olive oil
salt and ground black pepper

1 Put the potatoes in a large pan of lightly salted boiling water and cook for 15–20 minutes or until tender. Drain, cool slightly, then cut each into quarters lengthways and keep them warm.

2 Meanwhile, make the dressing. Put the capers, mustard and olive oil in a mini processor and blend until thick. Season well with salt and pepper.

3 Put the warm potatoes in a large salad bowl, add the dressing and tarragon and toss everything together.

4 Put the caperberries in the bowl with the potatoes and toss together.

Serves	EASY		NUTRITIONAL INFORMATION	
6	**Preparation Time** 15 minutes	**Cooking Time** 15–20 minutes	**Per Serving** 148 calories, 8g fat (of which 1g saturates), 18g carbohydrate, 0.2g salt	Vegetarian Gluten free • Dairy free

Asparagus, Pea and Mint Rice Salad

175g (6oz) mixed basmati and wild rice

1 large shallot, finely sliced

grated zest and juice of 1 small lemon

2 tbsp sunflower oil

12 fresh mint leaves, roughly chopped, plus extra sprigs to garnish

150g (5oz) asparagus tips

75g (3oz) fresh or frozen peas

salt and ground black pepper

1 Put the rice in a pan with twice its volume of water and a pinch of salt. Cover and bring to the boil. Reduce the heat to very low and cook according to the packet instructions. Once cooked, tip the rice on to a baking sheet and spread out to cool quickly. When cool, spoon into a large bowl.

2 In a small bowl, mix the shallot with the lemon zest and juice, oil and chopped mint, then stir into the rice.

3 Bring a large pan of lightly salted water to the boil. Add the asparagus and peas and cook for 3–4 minutes until tender. Drain and refresh in a bowl of cold water. Drain well and stir into the rice. Put into a serving dish and garnish with mint sprigs.

EASY	NUTRITIONAL INFORMATION		Serves
Preparation Time 10 minutes	**Cooking Time** 20 minutes	**Per Serving** 157 calories, 4g fat (of which trace saturates), 26g carbohydrate, trace salt	Vegetarian Gluten free • Dairy free	**6**

Try Something Different

Thai-style Coleslaw: replace the red cabbage with a good handful of fresh bean sprouts, the parsley with freshly chopped coriander, and add 1 seeded and finely chopped red chilli (see page 64). For the dressing, replace the vinegar with lime juice, the olive oil with toasted sesame oil and the mustard with soy sauce.

Classic Coleslaw

¼ each medium red and white cabbage, shredded

1 carrot, grated

20g (¾ oz) flat-leafed parsley, finely chopped

For the dressing

1½ tbsp red wine vinegar

4 tbsp olive oil

½ tsp Dijon mustard

salt and ground black pepper

1 To make the dressing, put the vinegar in a small bowl, add the olive oil and mustard, season well with salt and pepper and mix well.

2 Put the cabbage and carrot into a large bowl and toss to mix well. Add the parsley.

3 Mix the dressing again, pour over the cabbage mixture and toss well to coat.

Serves 6	EASY	NUTRITIONAL INFORMATION	
	Preparation Time 15 minutes	Per Serving 92 calories, 8g fat (of which 1g saturates), 5g carbohydrate, 0.1g salt	Vegetarian Gluten free • Dairy free

75g (3oz) lamb's lettuce

1 small head radicchio

2 small chicory heads

75g (3oz) walnuts, toasted and roughly chopped

For the dressing

2 tbsp white wine vinegar

2 tbsp walnut oil

4 tbsp olive oil

salt and ground black pepper

Winter Leaf Salad

1 To make the dressing, put all the ingredients in a jug. Season with salt and pepper and mix well.

2 Tear all the salad leaves into bite-size pieces and put into a large bowl. Add the walnuts and toss to mix. Mix the dressing again, pour it over the salad and toss well.

EASY		NUTRITIONAL INFORMATION		Serves
Preparation Time 10 minutes	**Cooking Time** 2 minutes	**Per Serving** 196 calories, 20g fat (of which 2g saturates), 2g carbohydrate, 0.6g salt	Vegetarian Gluten free • Dairy free	**6**

3

Fish and Shellfish

Warm Mussel, Leek and Herb Salad

700g (1½lb) trimmed baby leeks

juice of 1 lemon

½ tsp Dijon mustard

6 tbsp olive oil

4 tbsp roughly chopped fresh chervil or parsley

2 tbsp freshly chopped chives

900g (2lb) cooked mussels in the shell (see Cook's Tip)

salt and ground black pepper

orange wedges to garnish

1 Cook the leeks in salted boiling water until just tender. Drain and refresh in iced water. Drain and dry well on kitchen paper.

2 Put 2 tbsp lemon juice in a bowl, season with salt and pepper and add the mustard. Whisk to combine, then whisk in the olive oil. Toss the leeks in a little of the dressing, then cover and chill.

3 Just before serving, mix the herbs into the reserved dressing. Reheat the mussels and pour the dressing over. Spoon the hot mussels over the leeks and serve garnished with orange wedges.

Cook's Tip

Ready-cooked, vacuum-packed mussels are available from most supermarkets.

EASY		NUTRITIONAL INFORMATION		Serves
Preparation Time 10 minutes	**Cooking Time** 5-10 minutes	**Per Serving** 250 calories, 19g fat (of which 3g saturates), 5g carbohydrate, 0.4g salt	Gluten free • Dairy free	**4**

Cook's Tips

Chillies vary enormously in strength, from quite mild to blisteringly hot, depending on the type of chilli and its ripeness. Taste a small piece first to check it's not too hot for you.

Be extremely careful when handling chillies not to touch or rub your eyes with your fingers, as they will sting. As a precaution, use rubber gloves when preparing them if you like. Wash knives immediately after handling chillies for the same reason.

Chinese Prawn Noodle Salad

450g (1lb) straight-to-wok medium egg noodles

2 red chillies, seeded and finely chopped (see Cook's Tips)

4 spring onions, finely sliced

½ cucumber, halved lengthways, seeded and finely diced

350g (12oz) cooked prawns

1 tbsp freshly chopped coriander

For the soy and sesame dressing

2 tbsp runny honey

2 tbsp dark soy sauce

2 tbsp rice wine vinegar

4 tbsp sesame oil

ground black pepper

1 Put the noodles into a bowl and pour over boiling water to cover. Cover with clingfilm and leave for 5 minutes.

2 To make the dressing, whisk the honey, soy sauce, vinegar and sesame oil together with some black pepper. Drain the noodles and, while still warm, pour over the dressing. Toss together, then leave to cool.

3 To serve, stir the chillies, spring onions, cucumber, prawns and coriander into the noodles and pile into four bowls. If you have time, chill for 30 minutes– 1 hour.

Serves 4	EASY		NUTRITIONAL INFORMATION	
	Preparation Time 15 minutes, plus chilling and 5 minutes soaking		**Per Serving** 632 calories, 21g fat (of which 4g saturates), 88g carbohydrate, 2.2g salt	Dairy free

Cook's Tip

If you can't buy dressed crabs, use the same weight of frozen crab meat. Thaw at cool room temperature.

2 small dressed crabs, each with about 100g (3½oz) crab meat (see Cook's Tip)

2 tsp freshly chopped flat-leafed parsley

buttered grilled focaccia slices and rocket leaves to serve

For the orange vinaigrette

grated zest and juice of 1 orange

½ tsp Dijon mustard

2 tsp wine vinegar

6 tbsp olive oil

salt and ground black pepper

Crab and Orange Salad

1   To make the vinaigrette, put the orange zest and 4 tbsp orange juice in a small bowl with the mustard, wine vinegar, salt and pepper. Whisk together until thoroughly combined, then whisk in the olive oil.

2   Place the white crab meat in a small bowl and moisten with some of the vinaigrette; adjust the seasoning if necessary.

3   Put a slice of grilled focaccia on each plate. Spread the brown crab meat on the bread if you like, then spoon the white meat mixture on top. Sprinkle with the parsley and a little extra vinaigrette. Serve with the rocket leaves.

EASY	NUTRITIONAL INFORMATION	Serves
Preparation Time 20 minutes	**Per Serving** 862 calories, 45g fat (of which 6g saturates), 84g carbohydrate, 3.1g salt	**2**

Warm Prawn, Bacon and Mushroom Salad

175g (6oz) unsmoked streaky bacon, roughly chopped

75g (3oz) walnuts, roughly broken

3 tbsp olive oil

125g (4oz) shallots, finely sliced

2 garlic cloves, crushed

225g (8oz) brown-cap or chestnut mushrooms, thickly sliced

4 tbsp brandy

450g (1lb) raw prawns, peeled and deveined

250g (9oz) mixed robust salad leaves, such as frisée, escarole or radicchio

snipped fresh chives to garnish

For the dressing

1 tsp Dijon mustard

2 tbsp white wine vinegar

5 tbsp each walnut oil and olive oil

salt and ground black pepper

1 First, make the dressing. Whisk together all the ingredients in a small bowl, then set aside.

2 To make the salad, heat a heavy-based frying pan, add the bacon and dry-fry, stirring, for 5 minutes. Add the walnuts and cook for 2–3 minutes until crisp. Drain and set aside. Wipe the pan with kitchen paper.

3 Heat the oil in the wiped-out pan, add the shallots and cook, stirring, for 5 minutes. Add the garlic and mushrooms and fry for 2–3 minutes. Add the brandy and reduce for 1–2 minutes until syrupy. Add the prawns and stir-fry over a high heat for 2 minutes or until pink. Add the bacon.

4 Toss the salad leaves with half the dressing and arrange on six plates. Add the remaining dressing to the prawn mixture and spoon on top of the salad. Garnish with chives and serve immediately.

Try Something Different

Warm Scallop, Chorizo and Courgette Salad: replace the bacon with chopped chorizo, the walnuts with pinenuts, the mushrooms with 2 courgettes, halved lengthways and sliced diagonally, and the prawns with fresh raw scallops.

Serves	EASY		NUTRITIONAL INFORMATION	
6	**Preparation Time** 20 minutes	**Cooking Time** 20 minutes	**Per Serving** 459 calories, 37g fat (of which 6g saturates), 3g carbohydrate, 1.3g salt	Gluten free • Dairy free

Smoked Trout, Tomato and Lemon Salad

4 ripe tomatoes, sliced

caster sugar to sprinkle

5 tbsp crème fraiche

2 tbsp horseradish cream

2 tbsp dill and mustard sauce

grated zest of ½ lemon and 2 tbsp lemon juice

275g (10oz) smoked trout fillets, flaked

4 thick slices country-style bread

1 Little Gem lettuce, separated into small leaves

salt and ground black pepper

lemon wedges to serve

1 Put the tomato slices on a plate and season with a little sugar, salt and pepper. Cover and put to one side.

2 Put the crème fraîche, horseradish cream, dill and mustard sauce, lemon zest and juice in a large bowl. Whisk together and season with salt and pepper.

3 Add the smoked trout to the crème fraîche mixture and toss together.

4 Toast the bread lightly on both sides. Put a slice of toast on each of four serving plates. Arrange the tomato on top of the toast; spoon over any tomato juice. Arrange the lettuce and the trout mixture on top of the tomato, and serve with the lemon wedges.

Serves	EASY		NUTRITIONAL INFORMATION
4	**Preparation Time** 20 minutes	**Cooking Time** 3 minutes	**Per Serving** 295 calories, 14g fat (of which 7g saturates), 20g carbohydrate, 4.3g salt

Couscous and Haddock Salad

175g (6oz) couscous

125g (4oz) cooked smoked haddock, flaked

50g (2oz) cooked peas

a pinch of curry powder

2 spring onions, sliced

1 tbsp freshly chopped flat-leafed parsley

1 small hard-boiled egg, chopped

2 tbsp olive oil

2 tsp lemon juice

salt and ground black pepper

1 Cook the couscous according to the packet instructions. Drain if necessary.

2 Mix the couscous with the smoked haddock, peas, curry powder, spring onions, parsley and egg.

3 Toss with the olive oil, lemon juice and plenty of salt and pepper to taste, then serve.

EASY		NUTRITIONAL INFORMATION		Serves
Preparation Time 15 minutes	**Cooking Time** 15 minutes	**Per Serving** 408 calories, 15g fat (of which 2g saturates), 48g carbohydrate, 1.3g salt	Dairy free	**4**

Trout with Apple and Watercress Salad

4 x 150g (5oz) trout fillets
1 tbsp olive oil, plus extra to grease
250g (9oz) cooked baby new potatoes, cut into chunks
2 apples, cored and cut into chunks
4 cooked beetroot (not in vinegar), cut into chunks
150g (5oz) watercress
salt and ground black pepper

For the dressing
1 tbsp extra virgin olive oil
juice of ½ lemon
2 tsp Dijon mustard
1 tbsp freshly chopped dill

1 Preheat the oven to 200°C (180°C fan oven) mark 6. Put each piece of fish on a piece of greased foil, brush the top of the fish with olive oil and season with salt and pepper. Scrunch the foil around the fish and roast for 15–20 minutes until the fish is cooked.

2 Put the potatoes, apples, beetroot and watercress into a large bowl and mix together lightly.

3 Mix all the dressing ingredients together in a small bowl and season with salt and pepper. Toss through the salad, then serve with the fish.

Serves 4	EASY		NUTRITIONAL INFORMATION	
	Preparation Time 15 minutes	**Cooking Time** 15–20 minutes	**Per Serving** 320 calories, 12g fat (of which 1g saturates), 21g carbohydrate, 0.4g salt	Gluten free • Dairy free

1kg (2¼lb) new potatoes

8 gherkins, thinly sliced

2 x 280g tubs sweet cured herrings, drained, sliced into 2cm (¾ in) strips

For the soured cream dressing

2 tbsp soured cream

6 tbsp mayonnaise

2 tbsp freshly chopped dill

salt and ground black pepper

Marinated Herring, Potato and Dill Salad

1 Put the potatoes into a pan of cold water, bring to the boil and cook for 15–20 minutes until tender. Drain, then cut in half.

2 Meanwhile, make the dressing. Mix the soured cream, mayonnaise and dill together in a large bowl. Season well with salt and pepper.

3 To assemble the salad, put the potatoes, gherkins and herrings in a bowl with the dressing and toss together. Check the seasoning and serve.

EASY		NUTRITIONAL INFORMATION		Serves
Preparation Time 15 minutes	**Cooking Time** 15–20 minutes	**Per Serving** 610 calories, 33g fat (of which 4g saturates), 54g carbohydrate, 2.9g salt	Gluten free	**4**

Cook's Tip

Buy tuna steak canned in olive oil, which breaks easily into large, meaty flakes and has a good flavour.

Tuna, Bean and Red Onion Salad

400g can cannellini beans, drained and rinsed

1 small red onion, very finely sliced

1 tbsp red wine vinegar

225g can tuna steak in oil (see Cook's Tip)

2 tbsp freshly chopped parsley

salt and ground black pepper

1 Put the cannellini beans, onion slices and vinegar into a bowl, season with a little salt and mix well. Add the tuna with its oil, breaking the fish into large flakes.

2 Add half the parsley and season generously with pepper. Toss the salad, then scatter the remaining parsley over the top.

Serves 4	EASY	NUTRITIONAL INFORMATION	
	Preparation Time 5 minutes	Per Serving 190 calories, 6g fat (of which 1g saturates), 15g carbohydrate, 1.1g salt	Gluten free • Dairy free

Smoked Mackerel Citrus Salad

200g (7oz) green beans
200g (7oz) smoked mackerel fillets
125g (4oz) mixed watercress, spinach and rocket
4 spring onions, sliced
1 avocado, halved, stoned, peeled and sliced

For the dressing
1 tbsp olive oil
1 tbsp freshly chopped coriander
grated zest and juice of 1 orange

1 Blanch the green beans in boiling water for 3 minutes until they are just tender. Drain, rinse under cold running water, drain well, then tip into a bowl.

2 Preheat the grill and cook the mackerel for 2 minutes until warmed through. Flake into bite-size pieces, discard the skin and add the fish to the bowl with the salad leaves, spring onions and avocado.

3 Whisk all the dressing ingredients together in a small bowl. Pour over the salad, toss well and serve immediately.

EASY		NUTRITIONAL INFORMATION		Serves
Preparation Time 10 minutes	**Cooking Time** 5 minutes	**Per Serving** 299 calories, 26g fat (of which 5g saturates), 4g carbohydrate, 1g salt	Gluten free • Dairy free	**6**

Warm Spiced Salmon Niçoise

350g (12oz) new potatoes, thickly sliced
175g (6oz) fine green beans, halved
175g (6oz) cherry tomatoes, halved
1 small red onion, cut into thin wedges
4 x 150–175g (5–6oz) salmon fillets, skinned
15g (½ oz) butter, melted
1 tbsp coriander seeds, crushed
½ tsp dried crushed chillies
4 tbsp Caesar Dressing (see page 25)
flaked sea salt and ground black pepper
fresh chives to garnish

1 Cook the potatoes in salted boiling water for 8–10 minutes until just tender, adding the beans for the last 2 minutes. Drain well, then transfer to a bowl with the tomatoes and the onion wedges.

2 Cut each salmon fillet into three strips. Place the strips in four piles on a baking sheet and brush each pile with the melted butter. Mix the crushed coriander seeds with the chillies and a little sea salt and sprinkle evenly over the salmon. Place under a hot grill and cook for 4–5 minutes until just cooked through.

3 Add 1 tbsp water to the Caesar Dressing to thin it slightly (it should be the consistency of single cream). Spoon three-quarters of the dressing over the vegetables and toss to coat. Season well.

4 Divide the vegetables among four serving plates, top with the salmon pieces and drizzle the remaining dressing around the edge of the salad. Garnish with chives and serve.

Try Something Different

The spiced topping can be used for other firm fish, such as sea bass or monkfish.

EASY		NUTRITIONAL INFORMATION		Serves
Preparation Time 15 minutes	**Cooking Time** 15 minutes	**Per Serving** 480 calories, 28g fat (of which 6g saturates), 18g carbohydrate, 0.6g salt	Gluten free	**4**

4

Poultry and Meat

Try Something Different

For a vegetarian alternative, replace the ham with 150g (5oz) Gruyère or Cheddar cheese, cubed.

Spicy Cumin Dressing: mix together 2 tbsp red wine vinegar, 1 tsp ground cumin, a pinch of caster sugar and 5 tbsp olive oil. Season to taste.

Apple, Chicory, Ham and Pecan Salad

450g (1lb) fennel bulb, halved

2 large Braeburn or Cox's apples, about 450g (1lb), quartered, cored and sliced

75g (3oz) shelled pecan nuts

300g (11oz) cooked ham, cut into wide strips

1 chicory head, divided into leaves

fresh flat-leafed parsley sprigs to garnish

For the poppy seed dressing

1 tsp clear honey

2 tsp German or Dijon mustard

3 tbsp cider vinegar

9 tbsp vegetable oil

2 tsp poppy seeds

salt and ground black pepper

1 To make the dressing, whisk together the honey, mustard, vinegar and seasoning in a small bowl. Whisk in the oil, then the poppy seeds. Put to one side.

2 Remove and discard the centre core from the fennel and slice the fennel thinly lengthways. Place the fennel, apples, nuts, ham and chicory in a large serving bowl. Toss with the dressing and adjust the seasoning if necessary. Garnish with parsley sprigs and serve immediately.

Serves 6	EASY	NUTRITIONAL INFORMATION	
	Preparation Time 15 minutes	**Per Serving** 340 calories, 28g fat (of which 3g saturates), 10g carbohydrate, 1.6g salt	Gluten free • Dairy free

6 duck legs, each about 200g (7oz)

1 tsp peppercorns

2 fresh thyme sprigs and 2 bay leaves

125g (4oz) pecan nuts

finely grated zest and juice of 2 oranges

225g (8oz) cranberries

125g (4oz) caster sugar

4 tbsp white wine vinegar

9 tbsp sunflower oil

3 tbsp walnut oil

125g (4oz) kumquats

salt and ground black pepper

salad leaves, such as frisée, to serve

Crispy Duck Salad

1 Preheat the oven to 180°C (160°C fan oven) mark 4. Put the duck legs in a large flameproof casserole, cover with cold water and bring to the boil. Simmer for 10 minutes, skim the surface of the liquid and add the peppercorns, thyme, bay leaves and 2 tsp salt. Transfer to the oven and cook for 45 minutes–1 hour until tender. Cool quickly in the liquid and chill overnight.

2 Put the pecan nuts on a baking sheet and toast lightly under a preheated grill.

3 Put the orange zest in a frying pan with 200ml (7fl oz) of the orange juice, together with the cranberries and sugar. Bring to the boil and simmer gently for 5 minutes or until the cranberries are tender. Drain the cranberries, reserving the juice, and set aside. Bring the juice to the boil and bubble until syrupy, then add the reserved cranberries. Set to one side.

4 Put a good pinch of salt and pepper in a small bowl, then whisk in the vinegar, followed by the oils. Cut the kumquats into quarters, then add to the cranberry mixture with the dressing and pecans. Set to one side.

5 Skim the fat from the surface of the jellied duck liquid and set aside. Cut the duck into thick shreds, leaving the skin on.

6 Just before serving, heat 1 tbsp reserved duck fat in a large non-stick frying pan and fry half the duck for about 5 minutes or until very crisp and brown; set aside in a warm place. Repeat with the remaining duck. To serve, carefully toss the duck with the cranberry mixture and serve with salad leaves.

A LITTLE EFFORT		NUTRITIONAL INFORMATION		Serves
Preparation Time 30 minutes, plus cooling and chilling overnight	**Cooking Time** 1½ hours	**Per Serving** 655 calories, 65g fat (of which 11g saturates), 22g carbohydrate, 0.2g salt	Gluten free • Dairy free	**8**

Spring Chicken Salad with Sweet Chilli Sauce

4 skinless chicken breast fillets, each cut into four strips

1 tbsp Cajun seasoning (see Cook's Tip)

2 tbsp groundnut oil, plus extra to grease

salt and ground black pepper

For the salad

175g (6oz) small young carrots, cut into thin matchsticks

125g (4oz) cucumber, halved lengthways, seeded and cut into matchsticks

6 spring onions, cut into matchsticks

10 radishes, sliced

50g (2oz) bean sprouts, rinsed and dried

50g (2oz) unsalted peanuts, roughly chopped

1 large red chilli, finely chopped (see page 64)

2 tsp sesame oil

Thai chilli dipping sauce to drizzle

1 Soak eight bamboo skewers in water for 20 minutes. Toss the chicken strips in the Cajun seasoning, then season with salt and pepper and brush with oil. Thread on to the skewers.

2 Place the skewered chicken fillets on an oiled baking sheet and cook under a hot grill for 3–4 minutes on each side or until cooked through.

3 Place all the salad vegetables, peanuts and red chilli in a bowl, toss with the sesame oil and season well with salt and pepper.

4 Divide the vegetables among four serving plates, top with the warm chicken skewers and drizzle with the chilli sauce. Serve immediately.

Cook's Tip

Cajun seasoning is a spice and herb mix including chilli, cumin, cayenne and oregano.

EASY		NUTRITIONAL INFORMATION		Serves
Preparation Time 15 minutes	**Cooking Time** 10 minutes	**Per Serving** 307 calories, 15g fat (of which 3g saturates), 8g carbohydrate, 0.2g salt	Gluten free • Dairy free	**4**

2 x 200g packs roast chicken

250g (9oz) baby leaf spinach

55g pack crisp bacon, broken into small pieces

For the dressing

grated zest of 1 lemon and 4 tbsp lemon juice

1 tsp caster sugar

1 tsp Dijon mustard

175ml (6fl oz) lemon-infused olive oil

4 tbsp freshly chopped basil

salt and ground black pepper

Basil and Lemon Chicken

1 To make the dressing, put the lemon zest and juice, sugar, mustard and oil into a small bowl and season with salt and pepper. Whisk thoroughly together and add the basil.

2 Remove any bones from the roast chicken, leave the skin attached and slice into five or six pieces. Arrange the sliced chicken in a dish and pour the dressing over, then cover and leave to marinate for at least 15 minutes.

3 Just before serving, lift the chicken from the dressing and put to one side.

4 Put the spinach in a large bowl, pour the dressing over and toss together. Arrange the chicken on top of the spinach and sprinkle with the bacon. Serve immediately.

Serves 4	EASY	NUTRITIONAL INFORMATION	
	Preparation Time 15 minutes, plus minimum 15 minutes marinating	**Per Serving** 331 calories, 25g fat (of which 5g saturates), 2g carbohydrate, 1.3g salt	Gluten free • Dairy free

Chicken Caesar Salad

2 tbsp olive oil

1 garlic clove, crushed

2 thick slices of country-style bread, cubed

6 tbsp freshly grated Parmesan

1 cos lettuce, washed, chilled and cut into bite-size pieces

about 700g (1½lb) cooked chicken breast, sliced

For the dressing

4 tbsp mayonnaise

2 tbsp lemon juice

1 tsp Dijon mustard

2 anchovy fillets, very finely chopped

salt and ground black pepper

1 Preheat the oven to 180°C (160°C fan oven) mark 4. Put the olive oil, garlic and bread cubes in a bowl and toss well. Tip on to a baking sheet and bake in the oven for 10 minutes, turning halfway through.

2 Sprinkle the Parmesan over the croûtons and bake for 2 minutes until the cheese has melted and the bread is golden.

3 Put all the ingredients for the dressing in a bowl, season with salt and pepper and mix.

4 Put the lettuce and sliced chicken in a bowl, pour the dressing over and toss. Top with the cheese croûtons.

EASY		NUTRITIONAL INFORMATION	Serves
Preparation Time 15–20 minutes	**Cooking Time** 12 minutes	**Per Serving** 482 calories, 27g fat (of which 8g saturates), 8g carbohydrate, 1.4g salt	**4**

Zesty Orange, Chicken and Tarragon Salad

350g (12oz) smoked chicken or cooked chicken breast, skinned and cut into long strips

2 oranges

2 large chicory heads, roughly sliced

50g (2oz) pecan nuts or walnuts, toasted and roughly chopped

For the orange and tarragon dressing

grated zest and juice of 2 oranges

2 tbsp white wine vinegar

1 tsp caster sugar

5 tbsp olive oil

3 tbsp freshly chopped tarragon

1 large egg yolk

salt and ground black pepper

1 To make the dressing, whisk all the ingredients together in a small bowl.

2 Put the chicken strips in a bowl, spoon over the dressing, cover and chill for at least 1 hour.

3 Remove and discard the peel and pith from the oranges, then cut into slices.

4 Place a layer of chicory in a large flat salad bowl and spoon the chicken and dressing over. Scatter on the orange slices and nuts and garnish with tarragon sprigs.

Get Ahead

Complete the recipe to the end of step 2, cover and chill separately overnight.
To use Complete the recipe.

Serves 4	EASY		NUTRITIONAL INFORMATION	
	Preparation Time 15 minutes, plus minimum 1 hour chilling		**Per Serving** 252 calories, 8g fat (of which 2g saturates), 20g carbohydrate, 0.5g salt	Gluten free • Dairy free

Chicken, Avocado and Peanut Salad

2 roast chicken breasts, about 250g (9oz) total weight,
skinned and sliced

75g (3oz) watercress

2 tbsp cider vinegar

1 tsp English ready-made mustard

5 tbsp groundnut oil

1 large ripe avocado, halved, stoned, peeled and
thickly sliced

50g (2oz) roasted salted peanuts, roughly chopped

salt and ground black pepper

1 Arrange the sliced chicken on top of the watercress, cover with clingfilm and chill until ready to serve.

2 Put the vinegar, mustard and oil together in a bowl, season with salt and pepper and whisk together. Add the avocado and gently toss in the dressing, making sure each slice of avocado is well coated.

3 Just before serving, spoon the avocado and dressing over the chicken and watercress. Sprinkle with the chopped peanuts and serve immediately.

Serves 4	EASY	NUTRITIONAL INFORMATION	
	Preparation Time 15 minutes, plus chilling	**Per Serving** 335 calories, 28g fat (of which 4g saturates), 2g carbohydrate, 0.1g salt	Gluten free • Dairy free

Try Something Different

For a less spicy flavour, replace the seasoned chicken with slices of smoked ham.

Cook's Tip

Jerk seasoning is a mix of Caribbean herbs and spices.

4 chicken breast fillets, skin on

4 tsp jerk seasoning (see Cook's Tip)

450g (1lb) Jersey royal potatoes

100ml (3½fl oz) mayonnaise

2 tbsp wholegrain mustard

2 tbsp vegetable oil

1 red onion, cut into thin wedges

125g (4oz) brown cap mushrooms, halved

225g (8oz) young spinach leaves

3 tbsp freshly chopped chives

lemon juice to taste

salt and ground black pepper

Quick Caribbean Chicken Salad

1 Season the chicken breasts and rub with jerk seasoning. Heat the grill to maximum. Grill the chicken breasts for 5 minutes on each side or until cooked through. Set aside.

2 Meanwhile, cook the potatoes in salted boiling water for 10 minutes or until tender. Drain, cool a little, then cut into chunks. Mix the mayonnaise and mustard together, then add to the potatoes, stir and set aside.

3 Heat the oil in a large frying pan, add the onion and fry for 5 minutes. Add the mushrooms and cook for a further 2 minutes, then season with salt and pepper.

4 Combine the potato and mushroom mixtures in a bowl and add the spinach. Toss with the chives, add the lemon juice and season with salt and pepper. Cut the chicken into thick slices on the diagonal and serve with the salad.

EASY		NUTRITIONAL INFORMATION		Serves
Preparation Time 10 minutes	**Cooking Time** 17 minutes	**Per Serving** 543 calories, 33g fat (of which 6g saturates), 25g carbohydrate, 0.7g salt	Gluten free • Dairy free	**4**

Cook's Tip

Jars of Italian marinated onions in balsamic vinegar are available in larger supermarkets and Italian delis.

Parma Ham, Onion and Rocket Salad

150g (5oz) Italian marinated onions, drained, reserving 1 tbsp of the marinade (see Cook's Tip)

4 tbsp olive oil

200g (7oz) rocket

8 slices Parma ham, about 100g (3½oz)

75g (3oz) Parmesan, pared into shavings with a vegetable peeler

salt and ground black pepper

1 To make the dressing, place the reserved marinade from the onions, the olive oil, salt and pepper in a bowl and whisk together until combined.

2 Put the onions in a large bowl with the rocket, Parma ham and dressing. Toss together and divide among four serving plates. Scatter the Parmesan shavings on top and serve at once.

Serves 4	EASY		NUTRITIONAL INFORMATION	
	Preparation Time 10 minutes		**Per Serving** 237 calories, 18g fat (of which 6g saturates), 4g carbohydrate, 1.4g salt	Gluten free

Get Ahead

Make the croûtons, then cool and place in an airtight container for up to one week. Grill the bacon, then cool, cover and chill for up to one day.
To use Place the croûtons on a baking sheet and warm in the oven at 200°C (180°C fan oven) mark 6 for 5 minutes. Complete the recipe.

Bacon, Parmesan and Anchovy Salad

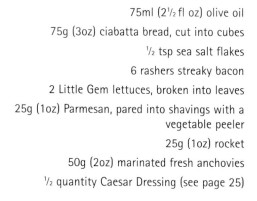

75ml (2½ fl oz) olive oil

75g (3oz) ciabatta bread, cut into cubes

½ tsp sea salt flakes

6 rashers streaky bacon

2 Little Gem lettuces, broken into leaves

25g (1oz) Parmesan, pared into shavings with a vegetable peeler

25g (1oz) rocket

50g (2oz) marinated fresh anchovies

½ quantity Caesar Dressing (see page 25)

1 Put half the olive oil in a frying pan and heat gently until a cube of bread sizzles. Add half the cubed bread and toss over the heat for 2–3 minutes or until golden. Remove with a slotted spoon and drain on kitchen paper. Repeat with the rest of the oil and bread, toss the croûtons in the salt and leave to cool.

2 Grill the bacon for 3–4 minutes on each side until golden and crisp. Drain and cool on kitchen paper, then roughly chop.

3 Toss the lettuce and Parmesan with the croûtons, bacon pieces, rocket and anchovies. Drizzle the salad with the dressing before serving.

EASY		NUTRITIONAL INFORMATION	Serves
Preparation Time 15 minutes, plus cooling	**Cooking Time** 15 minutes	**Per Serving** 339 calories, 26g fat (of which 6g saturates), 13g carbohydrate, 2.6g salt	**8**

Warm Bacon Salad

4 handfuls of soft salad leaves

1 small red onion, thinly sliced

75g (3oz) cubed pancetta

1 thick slice white bread, diced

2 medium eggs

25g (1oz) Parmesan, pared into shavings with a vegetable peeler

For the dressing

1 tbsp Dijon mustard

2 tbsp red wine vinegar

2 tbsp fruity olive oil

salt and ground black pepper

1 Put the salad leaves and onion in a large bowl. Fry the pancetta in a non-stick frying pan until it begins to release some fat. Add the diced bread and continue to fry until the pancetta is golden and crisp.

2 Put all the dressing ingredients in a small bowl, season with salt and pepper and whisk together.

3 Half-fill a small pan with cold water and bring to the boil. Turn the heat right down – there should be just a few bubbles on the base of the pan. Break the eggs into a cup, then tip them gently into the pan and cook for 3–4 minutes, using a metal spoon to baste the tops with a little of the hot water. Lift the eggs out of the water with a slotted spoon and drain on kitchen paper.

4 Tip the pancetta, bread and any pan juices over the salad leaves. Add the Parmesan, then pour the dressing over. Toss well, then divide between two plates. Top with the eggs, season to taste and serve.

EASY		NUTRITIONAL INFORMATION	Serves
Preparation Time 10 minutes	**Cooking Time** 10–15 minutes	**Per Serving** 375 calories, 29g fat (of which 9g saturates), 11g carbohydrate, 1.7g salt	**2**

Try Something Different

Use roast pork instead of beef.

150g (5oz) dried rice noodles

50g (2oz) rocket leaves

125g (4oz) sliced cold roast beef

125g (4oz) sunblush tomatoes, chopped

For the Thai dressing

juice of 1 lime

1 lemongrass stalk, outside leaves discarded, finely chopped

1 red chilli, seeded and chopped (see page 64)

2 tsp finely chopped fresh root ginger

2 garlic cloves, crushed

1 tbsp Thai fish sauce

3 tbsp extra virgin olive oil

salt and ground black pepper

Chilli Beef Noodle Salad

1 Put the noodles in a large bowl and pour boiling water over them to cover. Put to one side for 15 minutes.

2 To make the dressing, whisk together the lime juice, lemongrass, chilli, ginger, garlic, fish sauce and olive oil in a small bowl and season with salt and pepper.

3 While they are still warm, drain the noodles well, put in a large bowl and toss with the dressing. Leave to cool.

4 Just before serving, toss the rocket leaves, sliced beef and tomatoes through the noodles.

Serves 4	EASY	NUTRITIONAL INFORMATION	
	Preparation Time 15 minutes, plus 15 minutes soaking	**Per Serving** 286 calories, 11g fat (of which 2g saturates), 33g carbohydrate, 0.8g salt	Gluten free • Dairy free

Seared Beef Salad

1 tbsp sunflower oil

4 rump steaks

125g (4oz) crème fraîche

3 tbsp horseradish

a squeeze of lemon juice

100g (3½oz) baby leaf spinach

150g (5oz) radishes, sliced

8 cherry tomatoes, halved

225g (8oz) cooked new potatoes, sliced

salt and ground black pepper

1 Heat a frying pan over a high heat until hot. Add the oil and turn the heat down to medium. Season the steaks, then cook for 1½ minutes on each side for rare or 2 minutes on each side for medium, depending on the thickness of the slices. Cover loosely with foil and leave to rest for 5 minutes, then carve into thin slices.

2 Mix the crème fraîche with the horseradish, lemon juice and 1 tbsp warm water.

3 Arrange the beef slices in four bowls. Scatter with the spinach, radishes, cherry tomatoes and sliced potatoes. Drizzle with the horseradish sauce and serve.

EASY		NUTRITIONAL INFORMATION		Serves
Preparation Time 10 minutes	**Cooking Time** 3–4 minutes, plus 5 minutes resting	**Per Serving** 385 calories, 26g fat (of which 13g saturates), 13g carbohydrate, 0.5g salt	Gluten free	**4**

Thai Beef Salad

150g (5oz) chopped Chinese leaf or mixed salad leaves

1 large courgette, pared into ribbons

1 red pepper, halved, seeded and sliced

1 carrot, pared into ribbons

1 celery stick, sliced

1 tbsp each sunflower and sesame seeds, toasted

2 tbsp groundnut oil

1 tbsp sweet chilli sauce

1 tbsp soy sauce

juice of ½ lime

about 350g (12oz) leftover roast beef, carved into thin slices

1 Put the salad leaves into a bowl and add the courgette, sliced pepper, carrot, celery and seeds.

2 Put the oil, chilli sauce, soy sauce and lime juice into a small bowl and mix well.

3 Add the beef to the bowl. Drizzle the dressing over and toss well.

Serves 4	EASY		NUTRITIONAL INFORMATION	
	Preparation Time 15 minutes	**Cooking Time** 2 minutes	**Per Serving** 287 calories, 18g fat (of which 5g saturates), 8g carbohydrate, 1g salt	Gluten free • Dairy free

5

Vegetarian

Goat's Cheese and Walnut Salad

1 large radicchio, shredded

2 bunches of prepared watercress, about 125g (4oz) total weight

1 red onion, finely sliced

150g (5oz) walnut pieces

200g (7oz) goat's cheese, crumbled

For the dressing

2 tbsp red wine vinegar

8 tbsp olive oil

a large pinch of caster sugar

salt and ground black pepper

1 Whisk all the ingredients for the dressing in a small bowl and put to one side.

2 Put the radicchio, watercress and onion in a large bowl. Pour the dressing over and toss well.

3 To serve, divide the salad among six serving plates and sprinkle the walnuts and goat's cheese on top.

Serves 6	EASY		NUTRITIONAL INFORMATION	
	Preparation Time 10 minutes		**Per Serving** 428 calories, 41g fat (of which 10g saturates), 3g carbohydrate, 0.5g salt	Vegetarian Gluten free

Asparagus and Quail's Egg Salad

24 quail's eggs

24 asparagus spears, trimmed

juice of $\frac{1}{2}$ lemon

5 tbsp olive oil

4 large spring onions, finely sliced

100g (3$\frac{1}{2}$oz) watercress, roughly chopped

a few fresh dill and tarragon sprigs

salt and ground black pepper

1 Add the quail's eggs to a pan of boiling water and cook for 2 minutes, then drain and plunge into cold water. Cook the asparagus in salted boiling water for 2 minutes or until just tender. Drain, plunge into cold water and leave to cool.

2 Whisk together the lemon juice and olive oil and season with salt and pepper. Stir in the spring onions and put to one side.

3 Peel the quail's eggs and cut in half. Put into a large bowl with the asparagus, watercress, dill and tarragon. Pour the dressing over and lightly toss all the ingredients together. Adjust the seasoning and serve.

EASY		NUTRITIONAL INFORMATION		Serves
Preparation Time 30 minutes	**Cooking Time** 4 minutes	**Per Serving** 127 calories, 11g fat (of which 2g saturates), 1g carbohydrate, 0.1g salt	Vegetarian Gluten free • Dairy free	**8**

Cook's Tips

Peppadew peppers are from South Africa; sold in jars, they can be mild or hot.
Jalapeño chillies are from Mexico; they range from hot to fiery hot and when ripe they can be dark green or red; usually sold in jars.
Tahini is a paste made from finely ground sesame seeds. It is sold in jars.

Hummus with Rocket and Mint

3 tbsp sherry vinegar

75ml (3fl oz) extra virgin olive oil

150g (5oz) wild rocket

12 small fresh mint leaves

12 Peppadew sweet piquant peppers (mild)

6 tbsp sliced jalapeño chillies (see Cook's Tips)

sesame seed flatbreads and lemon wedges to serve

For the hummus

400g can chickpeas, drained and rinsed

juice of 1 lemon

4 tbsp tahini (see Cook's Tips)

1 garlic clove, crushed

75ml (3fl oz) extra virgin olive oil

salt and ground black pepper

1 To make the hummus, put the chickpeas, lemon juice, tahini, garlic and olive oil in a food processor. Season well with salt and pepper, then whiz to a paste. Spoon the hummus into a non-metallic bowl, then cover and chill overnight.

2 To make the dressing, mix the sherry vinegar and a pinch of salt in a small bowl, then add the olive oil and whisk to combine. Chill overnight.

3 To serve, divide the hummus among six (150ml/ ¼ pint) pots. Put on to six plates. Put the rocket and mint leaves in a bowl, then drizzle the dressing over. Divide the salad, peppers, jalapeño chillies and flatbreads among the six plates. Serve with lemon wedges.

Serves 6	EASY	NUTRITIONAL INFORMATION	
	Preparation Time 15 minutes, plus overnight chilling	**Per Serving** 399 calories, 30g fat (of which 5g saturates), 25g carbohydrate, 0.6g salt	Vegetarian Dairy free

Get Ahead

Complete the recipe up to the end of step 2, then leave the pears in the frying pan and set aside for up to 4 hours.
To use Warm the pears in the pan for 1 minute, then complete the recipe.

Warm Pear and Walnut Caesar Salad

50g (2oz) walnut pieces

1 tbsp walnut or mild olive oil

small knob of butter

3 firm rosy pears, quartered, cored and thickly sliced

1 bag Caesar salad with croûtons, dressing and Parmesan

100g (3½oz) blue cheese, such as Roquefort, Stilton or Danish blue, crumbled

1 bunch of chives, roughly chopped

1 Put the walnuts in a non-stick frying pan and dry-fry over a medium heat for about 1 minute until lightly toasted. Set aside.

2 Heat the oil and butter in the pan, then add the pears. Fry for 2 minutes on each side or until golden. Remove with a slotted spoon.

3 To serve, put the salad leaves into a large bowl. Add the walnuts, pears, croûtons, Parmesan and blue cheese. Add the salad dressing and toss lightly, or serve the dressing separately in a small bowl. Serve immediately, garnished with chives.

EASY		NUTRITIONAL INFORMATION		Serves
Preparation Time 10 minutes	**Cooking Time** 5 minutes	**Per Serving** 397 calories, 31g fat (of which 8g fat saturates), 19g carbohydrate, 1.3g salt	Vegetarian	**6**

Warm Lentil Salad

2 medium eggs
2 tsp olive oil
2 small leeks, chopped
4 spring onions, chopped
1 red pepper, seeded and chopped
400g can lentils, drained
150ml (5fl oz) vegetable stock
a handful of rocket leaves
salt and ground black pepper

1 Gently lower the eggs into a pan of boiling water and simmer for 7 minutes.

2 Meanwhile, heat the olive oil in a separate pan and fry the leeks, spring onions and red pepper for 6–8 minutes until softened.

3 Stir in the lentils and stock, bring to the boil and simmer for 1–2 minutes. Peel the eggs, then cut in half. Season the lentil mixture with salt and pepper, then divide between two serving bowls and top each with an egg and a few rocket leaves.

Serves 2	EASY		NUTRITIONAL INFORMATION	
	Preparation Time 15 minutes	**Cooking Time** 10 minutes	**Per Serving** 300 calories, 10g fat (of which 2g saturates), 33g carbohydrate, trace salt	Vegetarian Gluten free • Dairy free

Cook's Tip

Panzanella is a Tuscan salad, which uses stale bread.

Get Ahead

This salad is best made two or three hours ahead to let the flavours mingle.

Panzanella

2–3 thick slices from a day-old country loaf, about 100g (3½oz), torn or cut into cubes

450g (1lb) ripe tomatoes, roughly chopped

2 tbsp capers

1 tsp freshly chopped thyme

1 small red onion, thinly sliced

2 garlic cloves

2 small red chillies, seeded and finely chopped (see page 64)

4 tbsp extra virgin olive oil

125g (4oz) pitted black olives

50g (2oz) sun-dried tomatoes, roughly chopped

8 fresh basil leaves

25g (1oz) Parmesan, pared into shavings with a vegetable peeler

salt and ground black pepper

fresh thyme sprigs to garnish

1 Put the bread in a large bowl with the tomatoes, capers, chopped thyme, onion, garlic, chillies, olive oil, olives and sun-dried tomatoes. Season well with salt and pepper, then toss together and leave in a cool place for 30 minutes.

2 Toss the salad thoroughly again. Tear the basil into pieces and scatter over the salad with the Parmesan shavings. Garnish with thyme sprigs, then serve.

EASY	NUTRITIONAL INFORMATION		Serves
Preparation Time 20 minutes, plus 30 minutes chilling	**Per Serving** 228 calories, 14g fat (of which 3g saturates), 21g carbohydrate, 0.6g salt	Vegetarian	**4**

Roasted Vegetable Salad with Mustard Mayonnaise

900g (2lb) mixed vegetables, such as fennel, courgettes, leeks, aubergines, baby turnips, new potatoes and red onions

2 garlic cloves, unpeeled

4–5 fresh marjoram or rosemary sprigs

5 tbsp olive oil

1 tsp flaked sea salt

mixed crushed peppercorns to taste

4 tsp balsamic vinegar

warm crusty bread to serve

For the mustard mayonnaise

150ml (¼ pint) mayonnaise

2 tbsp Dijon mustard

salt and ground black pepper

1 Preheat the oven to 220°C (200°C fan oven) mark 7. For the vegetables, quarter the fennel, chop the courgettes, leeks and aubergines, trim the turnips and cut the onions into petals. Place the vegetables, garlic, marjoram or rosemary, the olive oil, salt and peppercorns in a roasting tin and toss well (see Cook's Tip).

2 Cook in the oven for 30–35 minutes or until the vegetables are golden, tossing frequently. Sprinkle the balsamic vinegar over and return to the oven for a further 5 minutes.

3 To make the mustard mayonnaise, mix together the mayonnaise and mustard, then season with salt and pepper and set aside.

4 Arrange the vegetable salad on a serving dish and serve with the mustard mayonnaise and crusty bread.

Cook's Tip

It's best to roast vegetables in a single layer or they will steam and become soggy. Use two tins if necessary.

Serves 4	EASY		NUTRITIONAL INFORMATION	
	Preparation Time 15 minutes	**Cooking Time** 40 minutes	**Per Serving** 420 calories, 43g fat (of which 6g saturates), 5g carbohydrate, 1g salt	Vegetarian Gluten free • Dairy free

Cook's Tip

Find marinated artichokes in supermarkets; alternatively, buy canned artichoke hearts, drain, slice and cover in olive oil. They will keep in the refrigerator for up to one week.

Grilled Ciabatta and Mozzarella Salad

8 thick slices Italian bread, such as ciabatta

2 tsp olive paste or sun-dried tomato paste

2 x 150g packs mozzarella cheese, drained and sliced

4 tbsp olive oil, plus extra for drizzling

2 tbsp balsamic vinegar

280g jar artichoke hearts in oil, drained and sliced (see Cook's Tip)

100g (3½oz) rocket salad

50g (2oz) sun-dried tomato halves

salt and ground black pepper

1 Toast the bread slices on one side. Spread the untoasted side with olive or sun-dried tomato paste, then top with mozzarella slices and drizzle lightly with olive oil.

2 Mix the vinegar, salt and pepper in a bowl and whisk in the 4 tbsp olive oil. Add the artichoke hearts.

3 Place the bread slices under a preheated grill for 2–3 minutes or until the mozzarella browns lightly.

4 Toss the rocket salad with the artichoke mixture and divide between four plates. Top with two slices of grilled bread and the sun-dried tomatoes.

Serves 4	EASY		NUTRITIONAL INFORMATION	
	Preparation Time 10 minutes	**Cooking Time** 5 minutes	**Per Serving** 613 calories, 33g fat (of which 13g saturates), 56g carbohydrate, 2.4g salt	Vegetarian

Cook's Tip

Halloumi is a firm cheese made from ewe's milk. It is best used sliced and cooked.

250g (9oz) halloumi, sliced into eight (see Cook's Tip)

1 tbsp flour, seasoned

2 tbsp olive oil

200g (7oz) mixed leaf salad

2 avocados, halved, stoned, peeled and sliced

fresh rocket leaves to garnish

lemon halves to serve

For the mint dressing

3 tbsp lemon juice

8 tbsp olive oil

3 tbsp freshly chopped mint

salt and ground black pepper

Halloumi and Avocado Salad

1 To make the dressing, whisk the lemon juice with the olive oil and mint, then season with salt and pepper.

2 Coat the halloumi with the flour. Heat the oil in a large frying pan and fry the cheese for 1 minute on each side or until it forms a golden crust.

3 Meanwhile, in a large bowl, add half the dressing to the salad leaves and avocado and toss together. Arrange the hot cheese on top and drizzle the remaining dressing over. Garnish with rocket leaves and serve with lemon halves to squeeze over.

EASY		NUTRITIONAL INFORMATION		Serves
Preparation Time 10 minutes	**Cooking Time** 2 minutes	**Per Serving** 397 calories, 34g fat (of which 13g saturates), 11g carbohydrate, 2.3g salt	Vegetarian	**4**

Warm Salad with Quorn and Berries

2 tbsp olive oil

1 onion, sliced

175g pack Quorn pieces

2 tbsp raspberry vinegar

150g (5oz) blueberries

225g (8oz) mixed salad leaves

salt and ground black pepper

1 Heat the olive oil in a frying pan, add the onion and cook for 5 minutes or until soft and golden. Increase the heat and add the Quorn pieces. Cook, stirring, for 5 minutes or until golden brown. Season with salt and pepper, place in a large bowl and put to one side.

2 Add the raspberry vinegar, 75ml (3fl oz) water and the blueberries to the frying pan. Bring to the boil and bubble for 1–2 minutes until it reaches a syrupy consistency.

3 Toss the Quorn, blueberry mixture and salad leaves gently together. Serve immediately.

Serves 4	EASY		NUTRITIONAL INFORMATION	
	Preparation Time 5 minutes	**Cooking Time** 12 minutes	**Per Serving** 152 calories, 7g fat (of which 1g saturates), 15g carbohydrate, 0.3g salt	Vegetarian Gluten free

Warm Tofu, Fennel and Bean Salad

1 tbsp olive oil, plus 1 tsp

1 red onion, finely sliced

1 fennel bulb, finely sliced

1 tbsp cider vinegar

400g can butter beans, drained and rinsed

2 tbsp freshly chopped flat-leafed parsley

200g (7oz) smoked tofu, sliced into eight lengthways

salt and ground black pepper

1 Heat 1 tbsp olive oil in a large frying pan. Add the onion and fennel, and cook over a medium heat for 5–10 minutes. Add the cider vinegar and heat through for 2 minutes, then stir in the butter beans and parsley. Season with salt and pepper, then tip into a bowl.

2 Add the tofu to the pan with the remaining olive oil. Cook for 2 minutes on each side or until golden. Divide the bean mixture among four plates and add two slices of tofu to each plate.

EASY		NUTRITIONAL INFORMATION		Serves
Preparation Time 10 minutes	**Cooking Time** 15 minutes	**Per Serving** 150 calories, 6g fat (of which 1g saturates), 15g carbohydrate, 0.8g salt	Vegetarian Gluten free • Dairy free	**4**

Thai Noodle Salad

200g (7oz) sugarsnap peas, trimmed

250g pack Thai stir-fry rice noodles

100g (3½oz) cashew nuts

300g (11oz) carrots, cut into batons

10 spring onions, sliced on the diagonal

300g (11oz) bean sprouts

20g (¾oz) fresh coriander, roughly chopped, plus coriander sprigs to garnish

1 red bird's eye chilli, seeded and finely chopped (see Cook's Tip and page 64)

2 tsp sweet chilli sauce

4 tbsp sesame oil

6 tbsp soy sauce

juice of 2 limes

salt and ground black pepper

1 Bring a pan of salted water to the boil and blanch the sugarsnap peas for 2–3 minutes until just tender to the bite. Drain and refresh under cold water.

2 Put the noodles into a bowl, cover with boiling water and leave to soak for 4 minutes. Rinse under cold water and drain very well.

3 Toast the cashews in a dry frying pan until golden – about 5 minutes.

4 Put the sugarsnaps in a large glass serving bowl. Add the carrots, spring onions, bean sprouts, chopped coriander, chopped chilli, cashews and noodles. Mix together the chilli sauce, sesame oil, soy sauce and lime juice and season well with salt and pepper. Pour over the salad, toss together, garnish with coriander sprigs and serve.

Cook's Tip

Red bird's eye chillies are always very hot. The smaller they are, the hotter they are.

EASY		NUTRITIONAL INFORMATION		Serves
Preparation Time 20 minutes, plus 4 minutes soaking	**Cooking Time** 7–8 minutes	**Per Serving** 568 calories, 29g fat (of which 4g saturates), 65g carbohydrate, 2.9g salt	Vegetarian Gluten free • Dairy free	**4**

6

Pasta and Beans

Pasta and Avocado Salad

2 tbsp mayonnaise

2 tbsp pesto

2 ripe avocados, halved, stoned, peeled and cut into cubes

225g (8oz) cooked pasta shapes, cooled

a few fresh basil leaves to garnish

1 Mix the mayonnaise with the pesto and avocados, then stir into the pasta. If the dressing is too thick, dilute with a little water (use the pasta cooking water if you have it).

2 Scatter a few basil leaves over the salad and serve as a starter.

Serves 4	EASY		NUTRITIONAL INFORMATION	
	Preparation Time 10 minutes		**Per Serving** 313 calories, 26g fat (of which 5g saturates), 14g carbohydrate, 0.6g salt	Vegetarian

Cook's Tips

To serve this dish hot, put 5 tbsp basil-infused oil in a frying pan, add the garlic and chillies and cook for 1 minute. Add the drained pasta and mix well, then add the tomatoes and mozzarella. Garnish and serve.
Instead of mozzarella, use Gorgonzola or Brie.
You can use 1/2 tsp dried crushed chillies instead of fresh.

2 tsp lemon juice

7 tbsp basil-infused olive oil

2 garlic cloves, crushed

350g (12oz) penne pasta

250g (9oz) mozzarella, cut into chunks

700g (1½lb) vine-ripened tomatoes, skinned, seeded and cut into chunks

½ large red chilli, seeded and finely sliced (see page 64)

½ large green chilli, seeded and finely sliced (see page 64)

salt and ground black pepper

fresh flat-leafed parsley or basil to garnish

Tomato and Mozzarella Pasta Salad

1 Put some salt and pepper in a small bowl, whisk in the lemon juice, followed by the flavoured oil and garlic, then set aside.

2 Bring a large pan of salted water to the boil, add the pasta and cook according to the packet instructions. Drain well, then tip into a large bowl and toss with 2 tbsp of the dressing (this will prevent the pasta from sticking together); set aside to cool. Put the mozzarella in a large bowl with the remaining dressing and set aside.

3 When ready to serve (see Cook's Tips), add the pasta to the mozzarella with the tomatoes and chillies. Toss together and season well with salt and pepper. Garnish with parsley or basil, then serve.

EASY		NUTRITIONAL INFORMATION		Serves
Preparation Time 20 minutes, plus cooling	**Cooking Time** 10–12 minutes	**Per Serving** 665 calories, 34g fat (of which 12g saturates), 70g carbohydrate, 0.7g salt	Vegetarian	**4**

Pasta, Salami and Tapenade Salad

3 x 225g tubs pasta salad in tomato sauce

75g (3oz) pepper salami, shredded

3 tbsp black olive tapenade paste

3 tbsp freshly chopped chives

salt and ground black pepper

1 Turn the pasta salad into a large bowl, add the salami, tapenade and chives. Toss everything together and season with pepper. Check for seasoning before adding salt – the tapenade may have made the salad salty enough.

2 Pile the salad into a large serving bowl. If not being served straight away, this salad is best kept in a cool place, but not chilled, until needed.

Serves 4	EASY		NUTRITIONAL INFORMATION	
	Preparation Time 5 minutes		**Per Serving** 332 calories, 20g fat (of which 6g saturates), 28g carbohydrate, 2g salt	Dairy free

Greek Pasta Salad

3 tbsp olive oil

2 tbsp lemon juice

150g (5oz) cooked pasta shapes, cooled

75g (3oz) feta cheese, crumbled

3 tomatoes, roughly chopped

2 tbsp small pitted black olives

½ cucumber, roughly chopped

1 small red onion, finely sliced

salt and ground black pepper

freshly chopped parsley and lemon zest to garnish

1 Mix the olive oil and lemon juice together in a salad bowl, then add the pasta, feta cheese, tomatoes, olives, cucumber and onion.

2 Season, stir to mix, garnish with chopped mint and lemon zest and serve.

EASY		NUTRITIONAL INFORMATION		Serves
Preparation Time 10 minutes	**Cooking Time** 20 minutes	**Per Serving** 382 calories, 27g fat (of which 8g saturates), 25g carbohydrate, 2.5g salt	Vegetarian	**2**

Red Pepper Pasta Salad

6 tbsp olive oil

1 garlic clove, crushed

2 tsp Dijon mustard

2 tbsp balsamic vinegar

350g (12oz) freshly cooked pasta shapes, drained

2 roasted red peppers, peeled, seeded and sliced

3 tbsp freshly chopped herbs, such as parsley, thyme or basil

salt and ground black pepper

1 Mix the olive oil with the garlic, mustard and balsamic vinegar in a small bowl. Stir into the cooked pasta and leave to cool.

2 Season with salt and pepper, add the sliced peppers and serve sprinkled with the herbs.

Serves 4	EASY	NUTRITIONAL INFORMATION	
	Preparation Time 10 minutes, plus cooling	**Per Serving** 275 calories, 18g fat (of which 3g saturates), 26g carbohydrate, 0.2g salt	Vegetarian Dairy free

Try Something Different

Replace the mixed seafood with 350g (12oz) cooked peeled prawns or 300g (11oz) smoked chicken, sliced.

Warm Seafood and Pasta Salad

175g (6oz) pasta shapes

3 tbsp olive oil

1 tbsp rice wine vinegar

grated zest and juice of 2 limes

2 red chillies, seeded and finely chopped (see page 64)

250g pack cooked mixed seafood

225g (8oz) yellow cherry tomatoes, halved

1 large avocado, halved, stoned, peeled and thickly sliced

1 red onion, finely sliced

50g (2oz) green olives

3 tbsp freshly chopped coriander

salt and ground black pepper

1 Bring a large pan of water to the boil, add the pasta and cook according to the packet instructions. Drain well, then transfer to a serving dish.

2 To make the dressing, whisk the olive oil and vinegar together in a small bowl. Whisk the lime zest and juice and the chillies into the dressing and season to taste with salt and pepper.

3 Stir the dressing into the pasta with the seafood, tomatoes, avocado, onion, olives and coriander. Stir well and serve immediately.

EASY		NUTRITIONAL INFORMATION		Serves
Preparation Time 15 minutes	**Cooking Time** 10–12 minutes	**Per Serving** 301 calories, 10g fat (of which 2g saturates), 36g carbohydrate, 1g salt	Dairy free	**4**

Pasta and Pastrami Salad

150g (5oz) cooked pasta, cooled
50g (2oz) pastrami, diced
2 tomatoes, chopped
½ cucumber, chopped
2 tbsp freshly chopped parsley
75g (3oz) red onion, finely chopped

For the dressing
wholegrain mustard to taste
4 tbsp Basic Vinaigrette (see page 24)

1 Combine all the ingredients for the salad in a salad bowl.

2 Mix the mustard into the Basic Vinaigrette, pour on to the salad and toss.

Serves 2	EASY		NUTRITIONAL INFORMATION	
	Preparation Time 10 minutes	**Cooking Time** 20 minutes	**Per Serving** 144 calories, 2g fat (of which 0.5g saturates), 24g carbohydrate, 0.8g salt	Dairy free

Get Ahead

Complete the recipe (but don't add the herbs or garnish), then cover and chill for up to two days.
To use Remove from the refrigerator up to 1 hour before serving and add the herbs. Garnish.

400g can mixed beans, drained and rinsed

400g can chickpeas, drained and rinsed

2 shallots, finely sliced

fresh mint sprigs and lemon zest to garnish

Mixed Beans with Lemon Vinaigrette

For the lemon vinaigrette

juice of 1 lemon

2 tsp runny honey

8 tbsp extra virgin olive oil

3 tbsp freshly chopped mint

4 tbsp roughly chopped flat-leafed parsley

salt and ground black pepper

1 Put the beans, chickpeas and shallots in a large bowl.

2 To make the lemon vinaigrette, whisk together the lemon juice, seasoning and honey. Gradually whisk in the olive oil and stir in the chopped herbs.

3 Pour the vinaigrette over the bean mixture, toss well, then garnish with the mint sprigs and lemon zest and serve.

EASY	NUTRITIONAL INFORMATION		Serves
Preparation Time 15 minutes	**Per Serving** 265 calories, 16g fat (of which 2g saturates), 22g carbohydrate, 0.9g salt	Vegetarian Gluten free • Dairy free	**6**

Warm Chorizo and Chickpea Salad

5 tbsp olive oil

200g (7oz) chorizo or spicy sausage, thinly sliced (see Cook's Tips)

225g (8oz) red onion, chopped

1 large red pepper, seeded and roughly chopped

3 garlic cloves, finely chopped

1 tsp cumin seeds

2 x 400g cans chickpeas, drained and rinsed

2 tbsp freshly chopped coriander

juice of 1 lemon

salt and ground black pepper

1 Heat 1 tbsp olive oil in a non-stick frying pan and cook the chorizo or spicy sausage over a medium heat for 1–2 minutes or until lightly browned. Remove the chorizo with a slotted spoon and set aside. Fry the onion in the chorizo oil for 10 minutes or until browned.

2 Add the red pepper, garlic, cumin and chickpeas to the onion and cook for a further 5 minutes, stirring frequently to prevent sticking. Remove from the heat and add the chorizo.

3 Add the chopped coriander, lemon juice and remaining olive oil. Season well and serve immediately.

Cook's Tips

Chorizo is a spicy Spanish sausage made from pork and paprika, which is available from most supermarkets and deli counters.

This salad is also delicious served cold.

For an extra kick, drizzle over 2 tbsp chilli oil.

To make your own chilli oil: put 8 fresh or dried chillies and 1 pint sunflower oil in a clean bottle, seal and leave for about two weeks. Strain into another clean bottle and use within six months.

Serves 4	EASY		NUTRITIONAL INFORMATION	
	Preparation Time 15 minutes	**Cooking Time** 17 minutes	**Per Serving** 583 calories, 39g fat (of which 10g saturates), 37g carbohydrate, 3.2g salt	Dairy free

Cannellini Bean and Sunblush Tomato Salad

½ red onion, very finely sliced

2 tbsp red wine vinegar

a small handful each of freshly chopped mint and flat-leafed parsley

2 x 400g cans cannellini beans, drained and rinsed

4 tbsp extra virgin olive oil

4 celery sticks, finely sliced

75g (3oz) sunblush tomatoes, snipped in half

salt and ground black pepper

1 Put the onion into a small bowl, add the vinegar and toss. Leave to marinate for 30 minutes – this stage is important as it takes the astringency out of the onion.

2 Tip the onion and vinegar into a large bowl, add the remaining ingredients, season with salt and pepper and toss everything together.

Serves 6	EASY	NUTRITIONAL INFORMATION	
	Preparation Time 5 minutes, plus 30 minutes marinating	**Per Serving** 163 calories, 8g fat (of which 1g saturates), 17g carbohydrate, 1.3g salt	Vegetarian Gluten free • Dairy free

Try Something Different

For a vegetarian alternative, skewer the whole tomatoes on soaked wooden kebab sticks, alternating with small mozzarella balls. Grill the kebabs and drizzle with 2 tbsp pesto sauce thinned with a little olive oil.

Spring Lamb and Flageolet Bean Salad

2–3 lamb fillets, about 700g (1½lb) in total

1 tbsp Dijon mustard

5 tbsp olive oil

1 tsp freshly chopped parsley

2 garlic cloves

juice of 1 lemon

400g can flageolet or cannellini beans, drained and rinsed

125g (4oz) frisée lettuce or curly endive

250g (9oz) baby plum or cherry tomatoes, halved

salt and ground black pepper

1 Rub the lamb fillets with the mustard and season with pepper. Put 1 tbsp olive oil in a non-stick frying pan and fry the lamb over a medium heat for 5–7 minutes on each side for medium rare, 8–10 minutes for well done. Remove the lamb, cover and set aside for 5 minutes. This allows the meat to relax, which makes slicing easier.

2 To make the dressing, put the parsley, garlic, lemon juice and remaining olive oil in a food processor and process for 10 seconds. Alternatively, put the ingredients into a screw-topped jar, screw on the lid and shake to combine.

3 Put the beans, frisée or curly endive and the tomatoes in a bowl, combine with the dressing and season to taste with salt and pepper.

4 Slice the lamb into 1cm (½in) slices and place on top of the flageolet salad. Serve immediately.

EASY		NUTRITIONAL INFORMATION		Serves
Preparation Time 5 minutes	**Cooking Time** 10–20 minutes, plus 5 minutes resting	**Per Serving** 535 calories, 35g fat (of which 11g saturates), 17g carbohydrate, 1.4g salt	Gluten free • Dairy free	**4**

Try Something Different

Use mixed beans, red kidney beans or chickpeas instead of cannellini beans.
Replace the turkey with cooked chicken.

Tarragon Turkey and Bean Salad

2 tbsp roughly chopped fresh tarragon
2 tbsp roughly chopped flat-leafed parsley
1 tbsp olive oil
2 tbsp crème fraîche
200ml (7fl oz) mayonnaise
juice of ½ lemon
450g (1lb) cooked turkey, cut into bite-size pieces
400g can cannellini beans, drained and rinsed
50g (2oz) sunblush or sun-dried tomatoes, roughly chopped
salt and ground black pepper
finely sliced spring onion to garnish

For the shallot dressing
2 tbsp sunflower oil
1 tsp walnut oil
2 tsp red wine vinegar
1 small shallot, very finely chopped
a pinch of caster sugar

1 Put the herbs in a food processor and add the olive oil. Whiz until the herbs are chopped. Add the crème fraîche, mayonnaise and lemon juice to the processor and season with salt and pepper, then whiz until well combined. Alternatively, chop the herbs by hand, mix with the olive oil, then beat in the crème fraîche, mayonnaise, lemon juice and seasoning. Toss the turkey with the herb dressing in a large bowl and put to one side.

2 To make the shallot dressing, whisk the ingredients together in a small bowl and season with salt and pepper.

3 Tip the cannellini beans into a bowl, toss with the shallot dressing and season well. Arrange the cannellini beans on a serving dish. Top the beans with the dressed turkey and the tomatoes, and garnish with spring onion.

Serves 4	EASY		NUTRITIONAL INFORMATION	
	Preparation Time 15–20 minutes		**Per Serving** 719 calories, 58g fat (of which 11g saturates), 13g carbohydrate, 1.5g salt	Gluten free

Glossary

Al dente Italian term commonly used to describe food, especially pasta and vegetables, which are cooked until tender but still firm to the bite.

Baking blind Pre-baking a pastry case before filling. The pastry case is lined with greaseproof paper and weighted down with dried beans or ceramic baking beans.

Baste To spoon the juices and melted fat over meat, poultry, game or vegetables during roasting to keep them moist. The term is also used to describe spooning over a marinade.

Beat To incorporate air into an ingredient or mixture by agitating it vigorously with a spoon, fork, whisk or electric mixer. The technique is also used to soften ingredients.

Bind To mix beaten egg or other liquid into a dry mixture to hold it together.

Blanch To immerse food briefly in fast-boiling water to loosen skins, such as peaches or tomatoes, or to remove bitterness, or to destroy enzymes and preserve the colour, flavour and texture of vegetables (especially prior to freezing).

Bouquet garni Small bunch of herbs – usually a mixture of parsley stems, thyme and a bay leaf – tied in muslin and used to flavour stocks, soups and stews.

Braise To cook meat, poultry, game or vegetables slowly in a small amount of liquid in a pan or casserole with a tight-fitting lid. The food is usually first browned in oil or fat.

Caramelise To heat sugar or sugar syrup slowly until it is brown in colour; ie forms a caramel.

Chill To cool food in the fridge.

Compote Fresh or dried fruit stewed in sugar syrup. Served hot or cold.

Coulis A smooth fruit or vegetable purée, thinned if necessary to a pouring consistency.

Cream To beat together fat and sugar until the mixture is pale and fluffy, and resembles whipped cream in texture and colour. The method is used in cakes and puddings which contain a high proportion of fat and require the incorporation of a lot of air.

Croûtons Small pieces of fried or toasted bread, served with soups and salads.

Crudités Raw vegetables, usually cut into slices or sticks, typically served with a dipping sauce.

Curdle To cause sauces or creamed mixtures to separate, usually by overheating or over-beating.

Cure To preserve fish, meat or poultry by smoking, drying or salting.

Deglaze To heat stock, wine or other liquid with the cooking juices left in the pan after roasting or sautéeing, scraping and stirring vigorously to dissolve the sediment on the bottom of the pan.

Dice To cut food into small cubes.

Dredge To sprinkle food generously with flour, sugar, icing sugar etc.

Dust To sprinkle lightly with flour, cornflour, icing sugar etc.

Escalope Thin slice of meat, such as pork, veal or turkey, from the top of the leg, usually pan-fried.

Fillet Term used to describe boned breasts of birds, boned sides of fish, and the undercut of a loin of beef, lamb, pork or veal.

Flake To separate food, such as cooked fish, into natural pieces.

Folding in Method of combining a whisked or creamed mixture with other ingredients by cutting and folding so that it retains its lightness. A large metal spoon or plastic-bladed spatula is used.

Fry To cook food in hot fat or oil. There are various methods: shallow-frying in a little fat in a shallow pan; deep-frying where the food is totally immersed in oil; dry-frying in which fatty foods are cooked in a non-stick pan without extra fat; see also Stir-frying.

Garnish A decoration, usually edible, such as parsley or lemon, which is used to enhance the appearance of a savoury dish.

Gluten A protein constituent of grains, such as wheat and rye, which develops when the flour is missed with water to give the dough elasticity.

Griddle A flat, heavy, metal plate used on the hob for cooking scones or for searing savoury ingredients.

Gut To clean out the entrails from fish.

Hull To remove the stalk and calyx from soft fruits, such as strawberries.

Infuse To immerse flavourings, such as aromatic vegetables, herbs, spices and vanilla, in a liquid to impart flavour. Usually the infused liquid is brought to the boil, then left to stand for a while.

Julienne Fine 'matchstick' strips of vegetables or citrus zest, sometimes used as a garnish.

Macerate To soften and flavour raw or dried foods by soaking in a liquid, eg soaking fruit in alcohol.

Marinate To soak raw meat, poultry or game – usually in a mixture of oil, wine, vinegar and flavourings – to soften and impart flavour. The mixture, which is known as a marinade, may also be used to baste the food during cooking.

Medallion Small round piece of meat, usually beef or veal.

Mince To cut food into very fine pieces, using a mincer, food processor or knife.

Parboil To boil a vegetable or other food for part of its cooking time before finishing it by another method.

Pare To finely peel the skin or zest from vegetables or fruit.

Poach To cook food gently in liquid at simmering point; the surface should be just trembling.

Pot roast To cook meat in a covered pan with some fat and a little liquid.

Purée To pound, sieve or liquidise vegetables, fish or fruit to a smooth pulp. Purées often form the basis for soups and sauces.

Reduce To fast-boil stock or other liquid in an uncovered pan to evaporate water and concentrate the flavour.

Refresh To cool hot vegetables very quickly by plunging into ice-cold water or holding under cold running water in order to stop the cooking process and preserve the colour.

Roast To cook food by dry heat in the oven.

Roux A mixture of equal quantities of butter (or other fat) and flour cooked together to form the basis of many sauces.

Rubbing in Method of incorporating fat into flour by rubbing between the fingertips, used when a short texture is required. Used for pastry, cakes, scones and biscuits.

Salsa Piquant sauce made from chopped fresh vegetables and sometimes fruit.

Sauté To cook food in a small quantity of fat over a high heat, shaking the pan constantly – usually in a sauté pan (a frying pan with straight sides and a wide base).

Scald To pour boiling water over food to clean it, or loosen skin, eg tomatoes. Also used to describe heating milk to just below boiling point.

Score To cut parallel lines in the surface of food, such as fish (or the fat layer on meat), to improve its appearance or help it cook more quickly.

Sear To brown meat quickly in a little hot fat before grilling or roasting.

Seasoned flour Flour mixed with a little salt and pepper, used for dusting meat, fish etc., before frying.

Shred To grate cheese or slice vegetables into very fine pieces or strips.

Sieve To press food through a perforated sieve to obtain a smooth texture.

Sift To shake dry ingredients through a sieve to remove lumps.

Simmer To keep a liquid just below boiling point.

Skim To remove froth, scum or fat from the surface of stock, gravy, stews, jam etc. Use either a skimmer, a spoon or kitchen paper.

Steam To cook food in steam, usually in a steamer over rapidly boiling water.

Steep To immerse food in warm or cold liquid to soften it, and sometimes to draw out strong flavours.

Stew To cook food, such as tougher cuts of meat, in flavoured liquid which is kept at simmering point.

Stir-fry To cook small even-sized pieces of food rapidly in a little fat, tossing constantly over a high heat.

Sweat To cook chopped or sliced vegetables in a little fat without liquid in a covered pan over a low heat to soften.

Tepid The term used to describe temperature at approximately blood heat, ie 37°C (98.7°F).

Vanilla sugar Sugar in which a vanilla pod has been stored to impart its flavour.

Whipping (whisking) Beating air rapidly into a mixture either with a manual or electric whisk. Whipping usually refers to cream.

Zest The thin coloured outer layer of citrus fruit, which can be removed in fine strips with a zester.

Index